A DAMSEL FOR THE DUKE

A Thrilling & Witty Historical Regency Romance Novel

In the Arms of a Rake Series

Emily Higgs

This book is a work of fiction. Names, characters, businesses, organizations, places, events and incidents either are the product of the author's imagination or are used fictitiously. Any resemblance to actual persons, living or dead, events, or locales is entirely coincidental.

CONTENTS

1

Chapter One

Excerpt from the gossip section of "The Gazette"

The women of the ton are ecstatic about the next season, as the most eligible bachelor in London, Lord Percival Whitworth, heir to the dukedom of Whitworth, is said to have finally found the bride. After the crown prince's wedding, his closest buddy has chosen to settle down. The women had been waiting for this attractive and mysterious guy to arrive at the marriage market.

Along with Lord Percival Whitworth's acquaintance with the crown prince, the Whitworths are descendants of the royal family from centuries ago and have been able to maintain ties to the throne. And, with his younger brother Lord Cedric

Whitworth's political career on the rise, the Whitworths will make no mistake in selecting the ideal girl from the ideal family to become the future Duchess of Whitworth. All members of powerful families throughout Britain have begun plotting to impress the Whitworths in order to be a part of this privileged family.

The Gazette is interested to see which family will be successful enough to join the Whitworths. It will be the most interesting story to see which fortunate woman will be able to capture the attention of the guy with the black eyes of night.

***

Lord Percival Whitworth maintained an emotionless demeanor as his youngest brother Dominic read the extract from the Gazette, while his whole family waited for him to jokingly refute the news. But the denial never came, and everyone understood it was best to stay quiet in front of the oldest Whitworth, with the exception of Lord Octavian, the third Whitworth brother.

"So, you have decided to willingly sacrifice yourself to those vultures," Octavian replied, chewing into his muffin.

"Be quiet, Tavi; it is time for all of you to start looking for nice women and marry them. I am quite thrilled, Percival. I believed I would never be able to play with my own grandkids. I was scared I'd never be able to talk about my gorgeous grandkids at those monthly tea parties," Lady Seraphina remarked reassured. "We should invite all our friends and their daughters to supper. I heard Isabella's kid had lately made her debut in society."

"Mother, please calm down. Let us depart for our estates, and then you may prepare as many soirees as you want, invite as many girls as you want to sacrifice your firstborn son," Dominic remarked, laughing.

"I would have been happy if you would really leave for your estate but all of us know you, Tavi and Felix are going philandering," the lord added with a sneer. "By the by Felix, how is Addie?" Lord Whitworth addressed his query at Felix.

"I don't know, Uncle. I'm thinking about going home this season." Felix remarked, "I don't want my mother to point a gun at my head because I haven't visited her in a long time."

"Oh, we haven't visited Donovan's estate in a long time either. We should spend this Christmas at Donovan Manor. Hopefully with a daughter-in-law," Lady Seraphina said hopefully.

"Marvelous idea mother," Dom remarked agreeably, "Percival will need a respite from signing innumerable dance cards in the season and Cedric's brain will also need rest from spending too much time on political nonsense."

While everyone was talking about Donovan's estate and getting ready for their vacation, the matter of Percival's bride was put to the back of their thoughts. Cedric planned to take over as leader of the liberal party shortly, and he was going to be his brother's shadow, leaving little space for error while looking for the future Duchess of Whitworth.

***

Percival has gone to every great ball in London, trying to locate the right woman to become the next Duchess of Whitworth. He did identify some debutantes who would make ideal duchesses, but they were too arrogant and uninteresting.

He didn't stop looking for a spouse for a month throughout the season. After all, as the oldest of Whitworth, it was his responsibility to provide for the successors, but he was on the edge of losing his mind over the same tedious chat with eager ladies and their moms.

He should thank his fortunate stars that no debutante has attempted to trap him in an undesired marriage. As humiliating as it was, he always retained a chaperone to prevent the debutante from assaulting him directly. His younger brother, Cedric, understood his plight better than anybody else and was usually with him.

Cedric had lately gained fame as a lawmaker in Parliament. Any incident not only tarnishes his family's reputation, but it also harms his career. It was critical for him to protect his family's image. It was now up to Percival to choose the least boring woman to marry and put an end to this ordeal before someone tried to create a scandal out of the Whitworth name.

"Lord Whitworth, how do you find this evening?" Lord Blackwood inquired, a young girl standing alongside him, ready to be introduced.

It has become commonplace; even conversations with men now consist in one of them introducing Percival to another woman, usually one of their sisters or distant relatives. Every young girl over the age of 17 from throughout the United Kingdom seems to have come to London this season to ensnare England's most eligible bachelor.

"Wonderful, the host hasn't spared anything for the celebration," he said, waiting for Lord Blackwood to complete his introductions.

"I would like to introduce you to my niece, Miss Rosalind Blackwood," Lord Blackwood said without spending time on trivial conversation.

Miss Blackwood performed the proper curtsy and began fluttering her eyelashes, which were meant to be captivating, but all Percival wanted to do was run and never look at another woman. Nonetheless, he fulfilled his obligations.

"I wonder if your dance card has an empty spot for me, Miss Blackwood," he added in his most appealing tone.

Miss Blackwood's face was already coated in an artificial blush on her cheeks, so he had no idea whether she got red.

"My next dance is available, my lord," she said promptly.

It's her first season then! Percival learnt all of the woman's strategies and tactics for catching his attention. The students who gazed at him with hero worship in their eyes and promptly responded to his request were only out of the classroom for their first or second ball. Those that took the effort to offer him another spot on the dance card and appear more controlled had varying experiences in the ballroom depending on how many seasons they went.

Along with subtle signs of waiting for a proposal from bachelor ladies, there was a rise in the number of offers for the position of his mistresses. He didn't understand why the married women of the ton were interested in him. And the widows were the most hazardous species he encountered. The person who is unconcerned about their reputation puts them in a compromising situation.

"Well, I would claim your next dance then, do excuse us, Lord Blackwood," Percival replied, taking the lady's hand.

The dance with the women was always the same. Same hesitant smiles, same discourse, and similar steps. The desire for a trip in only the first month of the season was overpowering. If he didn't receive a break, he may contemplate being a bachelor for the rest of his life, which would be unpleasant for many people, including his mother.

He often wished he could live like his younger brothers Dominic and Octavian, who do not have the responsibility of carrying the heir. They may choose to remain bachelors if they so like, but their mother will not sit quietly, even if one of her children is single.

The following morning, the Whitworths began preparations to go to the Duchy of Donovan for Christmas. Percival was well aware that when he returned to London after the new year, he would be announcing his engagement to the least dull woman he had encountered. So, he began building a list of all the females he had been introduced to so far with the idea of marrying. The study door opened, revealing Lady Seraphina.

"Ah! There's my boy."

"Is everything alright mother? Do you need any help?" Percival inquired.

"I have been the Duchess of Whitworth for so long, I do not need help with anything," Lady Seraphina stated, sitting in front of Percival, "But I have also been a mother for so long. When one of my sons needs assistance, I will be there, even if they do not ask this old woman."

"Mother, you know we won't hesitate to ask you if we need anything," he remarked, his whole attention on his mother.

"Being a mother also means realizing the woes of our children before they do."

He grinned at his mother, knowing full well that you can never win with the Duchess of Whitworth, even her political son Cedric.

"How about you just tell me the solution to my dilemma, mother?"

"I wish I had a solution to your difficulty, son, but I don't, so I've come here to reassure you that everything is OK. I understand that as the oldest of Whitworth, you have placed a lot of responsibility on yourself to follow in your predecessors' footsteps. However, marriage is not about selecting someone who precisely fits into society's expectations. If you want to marry, do it for yourself, the one who will accompany you through heaven and hell side by side. Percival, society and I will attempt to promote the ladies we believe are great for you, but it will be up to you to decide who you want to spend your whole life with."

"I'll keep that in mind, mom. Thank you," he said, beaming warmly at his mother.

"By the way, forget about bride searching over the holidays. Relax and enjoy yourself," Lady Seraphina murmured as she walked toward the door.

"Think about Addie, too. All of us adore her, and I believe she will make you an excellent wife," Lady Seraphina continued as she exited, giggling to herself.

2

Chapter Two

The Donovans were great friends with the Whitworths. Lord Whitworth and Maxwell Donovan, Duke of Harrington, were close friends who attended Eton and Oxford together. Lady Genevieve Donovan and Lady Seraphina Whitworth became close friends as debutantes. Their family was very close, and Felix, Tavi, and Dom were inseparable.

Felix was Lord Donovan's only child and spent all of his time with Octavian and Dominic. If Felix hadn't looked so different from Whitworth, he would have been mistaken for one of their brothers. They are approximately the same age and are known as Trinity by the ton because of their shared passion for chasing skirts all across Britain.

As planned, the Whitworths were on their way to Donovan Manor for Christmas. The bus trip to Donovan Estate was monotonous, and the weather outside didn't help; a storm was forming. The whole drive was unremarkable owing to the absence of the younger Whitworths, Dominic and Octavian, who constantly poked fun at one another and entertained everyone. But they had already departed with Felix to prevent Aunt Genevieve from killing him.

Seraphina spent part of the ride talking about one woman or the other, as well as the thrill of Percival's forthcoming wedding. He would never know if his father was snoozing or pretending to be asleep. Cedric continued to examine his reports, leaving Percival at the whim of his mother, who raved about ideal debutantes. He can't wait to go to Donovan's mansion and sleep away his ennui.

As Lady Genevieve urged Percival to assist Lady Adelaide with the placement of volumes in the library, all hopes of finding relaxation after arriving at the destination vanished. Lady Genevieve and Lady Seraphina's frantic endeavor to match Addie and Percival was not missed on anybody at the house.

"Library! I cannot believe our mother couldn't think of anything better than this," Octavian entered the library with Dom and Felix, asking, "Where is Addie, by the way?"

"She will be coming here any minute, she must be embarrassed already with the stunt mother and aunt pulled," Percival stated with a sigh, "You three, leave before she comes."

"Protective of your future wife already, eh," Dom replied, taking a book from the box. "I feel sorry for all the ladies waiting for you in London."

"Get out, now," Percival growled. They left him standing, annoyed, after mocking him endlessly.

As soon as the Trinity departed, Lady Adelaide, or Addie as she was known, entered the library. She was the daughter of the late Earl of Montgomery. Her parents died in an accident when she was 13, and she has resided at Donovan's estate as a ward of her Godmother, Lady Genevieve Donovan.

"Good afternoon, my lord," Adelaide said, "I hope you had a pleasant journey."

His mother's words echoed in his thoughts, and he looked at her differently than he had before. Percival saw how much she had grown since he last saw her. Her golden-brown hair seemed longer than he recalled.

"Quite the opposite, my lady," he answered tiredly.

"My Lord, if you are fatigued, kindly take a rest. I'll tell Aunt Genevieve and Aunt Seraphina that you helped me with the task," she remarked as she headed towards the crates of books on the floor.

"That won't be very gentlemanly of me now, would it?" He inquired, laughing.

"My Lord, I will keep your part of the work pending for you," she responded with a smile.

"Now that seems like a good bargain," he added with a chuckle. "I cannot believe elders are trying to match-make us."

"I cannot believe Lady Seraphina used such a desperate method, my lord", she remarked carefully placing books on the shelf, "But then again, this is my fourth season without a marriage offer and since you are also searching for a bride, it is natural they will try and match-make us."

Her grin faded. She was upset by the notion of remaining unmarried. She couldn't possibly remain at Donovan's forever as Lady Genevieve's ward, no matter how much they adored her as if she were their own child.

"I am not opposed to their idea of matchmaking us."

His remarks surprised her, and the book slipped from her grasp, dropping with a thump at her feet. She turned around and gaped at the guy standing in front of her, assessing her response.

"Are you jesting, my lord?" She accused, "Marriage is not a joke to me."

"I'm not joking, my lady; as you said, we're both seeking for marriage possibilities, so it's only right that we consider each other as such; I'll allow you to think about it. I will not court you without your permission;

have a good day," he remarked earnestly, making Adelaide consider marrying Percival Whitworth.

He always appreciated Adelaide's company when they visited Donovan's house. She never blabbered and always had something significant to say, which was seen to be unusual among women. She was also amusing at times, joining in Dom, Tavi, and Felix's jokes. Overall, she was an ideal woman to contemplate as his wife.

But the 12-year age disparity between them was disturbing for both of them. It was easy to marry an unknown debutante younger than her, but she made him nervous. She was just 20 years old, and he was a 32-year-old guy. Until now, he had never considered Adelaide romantically. She was quite young, but men married ladies who were older than them, and it was socially acceptable. He may be able to marry a lady who would not bore him to death after all.

The evening at Donovan Manor was pleasant, with everyone conversing and enjoying themselves over an intimate supper. Bennett's family, the sole local doctor, joined them, and they also had a daughter of marital age. But instead of him, she continued staring toward Cedric, which delighted Percival greatly. His brother seems threatening to everyone; ladies have never dared to look at him, and men have cowered in fear of him. His attention turned to Adelaide, who sat next his mother, listening intently as she looked extremely gorgeous. He was beginning to regret his spontaneous move in the library; he should have wooed her gradually.

Everyone was reclining in the parlor, chattering away, when it began to rain fiercely. Doctor Bennett and his family were unable to leave since it was pouring for hours. It was past midnight, and everyone had chosen to rest for the night when a footman rushed into the parlor, followed by a bedraggled, soaked mother carrying an unconscious kid in her arms.

"Doctor," the lady gasped, "p-please, p-please save him."

Everyone sprang up at once. Doctor Bennett went to the mother, carrying a kid in his arms.

"My lady, please send hot water immediately," Doctor Bennett half-ordered.

"Let's take him to the chamber," Lord Donovan remarked, leading the doctor to the second landing.

"Everyone, please stay here," Felix pleaded, half-running after his father. "I will take care of everything."

Mrs. Bennett spoke out after the guests had dispersed.

"Don't worry, there's no need to panic." Mrs. Bennett said, "My husband is very capable; he will ensure that nothing happens to the child."

"Yes, I have faith in Dr. Bennett," Lady Genevieve remarked, "Let us have some brandy till rest join us."

When everyone had settled down, Percival's gaze was drawn to the lady who arrived like a storm, water flowing off her, leaving a pool of rainfall around her while she gasped for oxygen in the corner of the parlour. He began to approach her when Lady Seraphina arrived first.

"Dear child, you are drenched, Addie ring for servants to bring blankets," she murmured.

"Do come near the fire, and have a sip of brandy, dear," Lady Genevieve said.

The lady blinked at the individuals in front of her, standing still. A second later, she realized and replied, "Thank you, my lady, but I am fine right here."

Everyone appeared perplexed by her unusual request.

"You will catch a cold," Adelaide complained.

"Who are you?" Mrs. Bennett inquired suspiciously at the same moment.

"Penelope Hawthorne, my lady," the woman said after a time.

Everyone saw Mrs. Bennett and Miss. Bennett's frightened scream.

3

Chapter Three

Her baby stopped wailing, and she worried when she saw his breathing was decreasing. When the carriage arrived in front of the Duke of Harrington's mansion, she leaped out and dashed inside.

"Miss! Wait!" the butler rushed up to her.

"I need to see a doctor right now," she said, "and the baby needs a doctor right now."

"Follow me!"

She rushed behind the butler without thinking.

"Doctor," she said as she entered the parlour, "please, please save him."

Everyone sprang up at once. Doctor Bennett ran to her, clutching the infant in his arms.

After the Duke of Harrington led the doctor to the second landing, she noticed she was soaked from head to toe, creating a pool of rainfall around her.

"Dear child, you are drenched, Addie ring for servants to bring blankets," Lady Seraphina remarked.

"Do come near the fire, and have a sip of brandy, dear," Lady Genevieve urged.

She realized she didn't know anybody other than Mrs. Bennett, not even Lady Harrington. Lord and Lady Harrington have made considerable gifts to the orphanage. They were the only reason the orphanage continued to operate. Lord Harrington even paid a few visits to the orphanage, but she was not permitted to be seen by the guests.

She realized that they had heard about her but never seen her. If they had known who she was, they would never have treated her so well. She spotted Mrs. Bennett looking at her. Because of her wet condition, it seems that the woman has not yet recognized her.

"Thank you, my lady, but I am fine right here," she responded in reply. It will not be nice if they discover who she is and toss her out without her child.

She nearly chuckled as everyone seemed perplexed by her words.

"You will catch a cold," a young woman warned, alarmed.

"Who are you?" Mrs. Bennett inquired at the same moment.

Fear gripped her. She would be asked to leave the moment her identity was exposed. For a minute, she pondered not giving her true identity, but then she would be labeled as a deceiver. And Mrs. Bennett was already suspicious.

"Penelope Hawthorne, my lady," she replied, attempting to seem brave despite the revulsion growing up within her for bearing the name of Britain's most notorious prostitute.

It answered some questions while further confusing others.

"What are you waiting for? Please provide the blankets at once." Lord Whitworth ordered the servants standing frozen at the entrance after hearing Penelope Hawthorne's name.

"Now come near the fire, child!" Lady Genevieve spoke with a tumbler of brandy in her hand.

She had no idea how she was compelled to sit in front of a fire, bundled in blankets, and drink brandy. The liquid burnt her throat, but she swallowed it down and soon felt warm from inside.

"Don't worry!" The doctor will take care of your child," Percival replied, his obsidian eyes grabbing her attention. "What is his name?"

"Ethan!" She said without thinking.

"Where is his father?" Cedric inquired. She realized he had the same eyes and features as the person sitting in front of her, but he was scarier.

"I don't know," she said coldly, her teeth trembling.

She understood what they were thinking. And yet, she did not attempt to dispel the myth; no matter what she does, she is evaluated wherever she goes. Everyone assumes she is the same as her mother, a whore.

But they knew very little about her!

***

Nell awoke to the sound of a rooster crowing in the early morning, like she does every day. She enjoyed the morning because it gave her the freedom to be herself without the scrutiny of the rest of the world.

It was still dark in the morning, but her task could not wait. It's the only thing maintaining the roof over her head and food in her stomach. She grabbed eggs for breakfast and began her daily activities. Children sleep late, but today a couple was coming to adopt a kid, so she would have to clean the office and make sure everything was acceptable, along with the children.

The remainder of the day was spent as normal, doing housework and caring for the children. She learned that the couple had opted to adopt Amelia, a six-month-old infant who had just arrived at the orphanage a month before. People who adopt generally rename the kid, but this does not imply they should be left unnamed. Some children, like her, are never adopted and may live their whole lives without a name. She wished she didn't have a name; it would have made things easy.

The evening brought a rain, delaying all of her chores. Children were terrified of the rain, so she had to put all of her work on hold until Mrs. Davies arrived and she could do the remaining duties.

Her life looked to be monotonous every day, but she was thankful since the alternative route she would have to take if she ever found herself unemployed would be worse than giving up her life.

She began heading toward the kitchen, the familiar cold stone under her feet, when she heard a baby wail somewhere near the door. She half-ran to see the door locked and a scream emanating from outside. Someone dropped another youngster on their doorsteps in the rain. She opened the door quickly, only to see a toddler almost drowned in the pool of water that had developed in his basket. She quickly snatched up the youngster and dashed to Mrs. Davies.

Nell cried, "Mrs. Davies, Mrs. Davies," as she ran into the corridor.

Mrs. Davies approached Nell with another youngster in tow.

"What happened, Nell? Are you okay?"

"Someone left a baby in the rain, look at him," Nell remarked, presenting the infant to Mrs. Davies.

"He's burning up. Cruel people! How could they abandon such an angel to die in the rain?" Mrs. Davies said, "We need to call a doctor right away."

"We'll waste a lot of time if we send for him; instead, I'll take him to Mr. Bennett personally," Nell remarked, stepping into the storage. "Ferdinand delivered the supplies today, so we still have his vehicle. I'll wake him up."

"I will wrap him in warm blankets, meet me at the front door with Ferdinand."

Nell stormed into the storage, dragging Ferdinand with her to get the carriage.

The orphanage was at one end of town, while the residence of Dr. Bennett, the town's lone doctor, was in the center, near the church. The cart was partially opened in the back, allowing the rain to reach Nell and wet her.

When they arrived to the doctor's home, they were informed that the family had gone to the Duke's house for supper and had not yet arrived. They began for the lone mansion at the opposite end of town, surrounded by acres and acres of the Duke's plantation.

***

As she stood there, everyone criticizing her for crimes she hadn't committed, the lovely guy in front of her looked at her without judgment, but compassion caused her heart to skip a beat. His obsidian gaze made her uneasy. They seemed like a vast, black hole from which she couldn't escape.

"She is not married, my lord," Miss. Bennett said with distaste in her voice to Cedric's query.

She knew this was the time when everyone around her would turn into petty, judgmental beings except when she glanced up, she couldn't see anything except pity in his dark eyes, which fueled her rage.

4

Chapter Four

The Whitworths and Donovans were enjoying a picnic at Donovan's private lake, which was close to the stunning stone edifice. Percival and Addie were once again secluded so that they could spend time together.

"What are you thinking about?" Percival inquired.

"The baby. I'm concerned about him. He wasn't in good condition when they left the manor, and we haven't heard anything about him since," Addie added, her gorgeous face filled with dread.

The doctor transferred the infant to his clinic the next day after treating him at the Manor and lowering his fever.

"I have been wondering about the same thing," Percival replied.

"Maybe we should go and visit the orphanage."

"Orphanage?" Percival inquired, confused.

"Percival," Tavi said from near the pond, "Help me. Dom and Felix are throwing me into the water."

Percival disregarded them as he usually does, well aware that if he attempted to assist, all three of them would turn against him. He moved away from the three monkeys to gaze at Addie, who was laughing at the catastrophe beside the pond. She looked lovely, with sunshine shining off her pale complexion and brown hair reflecting gold in the sunlight. He can't help but marvel how such a lovely woman has yet to get a marriage proposal.

"My lord, are you alright?" He found himself looking at her.

"When will you answer my question, my lady? We're both running out of time," Percival said plainly.

Addie pondered for a bit before responding.

"It should have been easy to answer you because I've known you almost my entire life, but I feel like I need to think about it more," Addie replied after a period of hesitation.

"Do you fancy someone?"

The question came out of nowhere, and for a brief minute, both of them were surprised.

"Uh," Addie faltered, and Percival understood she liked someone.

When she opened her lips to deny, he cut her off.

"Don't bother lying, Addie; your face said it all. So, who might be this fortunate gentleman?" Percival inquired jokingly.

"It is nothing, my lord, just a passing fancy," she replied with a stiff lip.

"Passing fancy!" He chuckled.

"Who?" He inquired again, smiling: "Your secret will be safe with me."

"Someone unreachable, my Lord," Addie said thoughtfully.

They went towards the mansion in quiet. Percival greatly loved Addie's agitated mood.

The atmosphere darkened when Lord Whitworth and Lord Donovan joined everyone and revealed that the orphanage had been demolished owing to rain.

"What about the children?" Dom asked.

"Daviess are unable to care for anybody longer. So, they will send the youngsters to the London orphanage, and the workers will be relieved." Lord Donovan explained.

"How is the baby?" Lady Genevieve inquired.

"Doctor is skeptical; he is doing his best but believes the child will not make it," Lord Donovan said.

"We should seek a better doctor from London," Tavi advised.

"Cedric, send the letter to Dr. Alexander. Tell him to come as soon as he receives the letter," Percival replied.

The infant died before the letter reached London. Everyone attended a little funeral ceremony for the youngster. And everyone quickly forgot about the youngster and returned to their nice holiday. The Whitworths considered Donovan to be another home, and they made the most of their time with their family.

Percival and Adelaide were spending more time together every day, which made everyone happy. They spent their time together in comfortable quiet, reminiscing about their upbringing. They knew they were compatible with one other, and if they chose to marry, they can see themselves developing a positive relationship and eventually becoming lovers. Until then, they will be excellent friends.

Percival was not troubled by Addie's affections for someone else, and he was not in love with her. For him, she was the ideal contender to become the future Lady Whitworth.

The parliament would be in session shortly, as would the brothels and gambling establishments. The Whitworth brothers were heading for London, the older two for parliament and the younger two for their exploits. The Whitworth parents stayed at Donovan's for the remainder of the season, joining their children for the season's final event, the "Prince's Ball".

The season begins with the "Queen's Ball" in honor of the queen and finishes with the "Prince's Ball," which declares the formal conclusion of the parliament session and is hosted by the prince and princess. Queen balls showcased grandeur and elegance, but Prince balls allowed the royal children to do anything they desired. To show respect for the royal family, the great houses of Britain do not hold balls before the Queen's ball or after the Prince's ball. Everyone else follows their example, retreating to their family estate for the remainder of the summer.

Percival had to accompany his closest buddy, the Prince of Wales, to the ball preparations, which consisted of little more than being present at court with his friend and saving him from his newly married wife. Cedric was elected to parliament as the Liberal Party's vice president. Octavian, Dominic, and Felix planned to go out with their pals and visit several brothels and gambling establishments.

Their belongings were packed and ready to go the following morning. Lady Genevieve learned of Mrs. Davies's request for an audience with her as the company was returning from their evening stroll.

"Is everything fine with Mrs. Davies, darling?" Lord Donovan asked his wife after supper.

"Yes, they relieved all of their staff and she actually came to ask if we can employ Miss. Hawthorne," Lady Genevieve said with a sigh. Donovan's family's expressions turned to pity.

"So, what is the issue?" Cedric asked the question that everyone was thinking about.

"What is it, Genevieve?" Lady Seraphina said, "She having a child out of wedlock cannot be the only reason."

"Seraphina, she doesn't have a child out of wedlock," Lady Genevieve said, perplexed by the inquiries.

"Then whose child was it?" Tavi inquired, surprised.

"Someone left the poor child in rain at the doorsteps of the orphanage, Miss. Hawthorne worked as a caretaker at the orphanage," the Lord replied.

"Then I do not see any problem at hiring Miss. Hawthorne," Percival went on to say.

"Do you know the infamous scandal of Nathaniel Cole, Lord of Greenville?" Lord Donovan said of his audience.

"Yes, that caused quite an uproar. I believe that was about the time Tavi was born. I recall Lord Cole being found guilty of killing a prostitute; her corpse was discovered in his bed, soaked in blood. It was terrifying to behold. It shook everyone at the time," said Lord Whitworth.

"Some people claimed Lord Cole was possessed by the devil," Lady Seraphina said.

"They termed it the Cole scandal. Lord Donovan says that the prostitute had a daughter from her prior unknown boyfriend before meeting Cole, whom she abandoned at an orphanage and named Penelope Hawthorne after herself." Everyone realized what had happened, and Percival couldn't help but feel protective of the lady. Her parents' sins were not hers.

"I still do not understand the problem," Dominic said.

"The difficulty is that everyone in the county is aware of her background, and no one wants to hire her. The orphanage owner had a difficult time because of her history, but since she was abandoned as a kid in their care, they also hired her," Lord Donovan stated.

"I won't mind taking her under my care, but I have a daughter that needs to be wed and I do not want to be any problem in her marriage because of the people we employ," she stated.

"Well, you shouldn't marry Addie to the family with such thinking," Tavi said with a smirk.

"It is not always feasible, son. Lord Donovan said that we must often consider the society in which we live, even if we dislike it."

"I believe we should engage her aunt," Addie stated. "She has nowhere to go. People created obstacles for the Daviess, but they did it nonetheless."

"We will think about it," Lord Donovan answered. "Let us enjoy the night." The talk quickly shifted to a new issue, with the notion of Penelope far from their thoughts.

Percival explained to his family that the crown prince is always on his toes since his wife is causing him problems. The crown prince married the princess of Spain last summer as part of a long-standing friendship arrangement between the two countries. And it was no secret that the princess was quite hesitant to marry a prince from a distant nation.

They were close to the royal family and knew practically everything that happened at the palace. They were, after all, heirs to the kingdom, and they discovered that being close to the reigning monarch had its own set of benefits and drawbacks.

5

Chapter Five

It's been a week. It took a week of hard labour to pack everything up and say goodbye to all of the youngsters. Goodbye to the only home she's ever known.

Nell was constantly afraid that she might lose everything; that her name and her mother's transgressions will send her to the streets. The apocalypse she knew would one day arrive, robbing her of whatever stability or dignity she had managed to preserve. The day she will have nothing as the claws of her mother's world attempt to pull her to hell. And she resolved that when the time came, she would rather end her life gladly than sell her body and be labeled a whore like her mother.

Her steely steel will to depart this planet corroded throughout the course of her existence. She was always aware that she was different from everyone else in her household and it took her a long time to understand that it wasn't her house, and the Daviess weren't her parents. When children of all ages arrived to the orphanage and spoke about their mothers and fathers, she was heartbroken since she had never known about her own blood. And when young infants were abandoned on their doorsteps because their parents did not want them, she assumed she was one of them. But when she got older and people chose everyone else over her, it crushed everything in her.

She requested that Mrs. Daviess, whom she referred to as Mama, tell her what was wrong with her. Was she unattractive, repulsive? Wasn't she a nice child? Mrs. Davies constantly told her that she was unique and a gift from God, and that one day she would have the finest family in the world, but for the time being, she would always have a home with them. She knew Mrs. Davies was pacifying her and keeping her hopes alive, so she willingly accepted the deception until that awful day when she discovered who she was and wished she hadn't.

She was just 15 years old and now worked with Davies's family to care for the children. She was content with her makeshift family, and she still called Mrs. Davies mother when no one else was there. Her chat with Mr. Davies was brief and to the point. She was playing with the kids when she heard the ruckus at the door. She shouted and yelled because she didn't understand. Mr. Davies's voice warned everyone that he will not allow anybody steal her. She wasn't sure who the folks had come for. As the shouts became louder, she gathered all of the children and led them to the basement where the food was stored.

She remained inside for a long time, her heart filled with terror but a great determination to protect the children. She refused to allow any of those guys touch a single kid. After a long time, she heard a tap on the door and Mrs. Davies's voice inquiring whether she was inside with the children. After feeding and putting all the children to bed, Nell saw Mr. and Mrs. Davies's disturbed and pale faces as they stared at everything except her.

Instead of sleeping, she went to Mr. Davies's office after hearing Mr. and Mrs. Davies's discussion muffled by the door. She knocked and entered the office when Mrs. Davies opened it for her. Pity and remorse flowed in their eyes.

"Nell," Mrs. Davies shouted, "Is everything well, child? Why aren't you sleeping?"

"Is it me?" She muttered, staring hopefully at the pair.

"She needs to know the truth," Mr. Davies said to his wife.

"No," Mrs. Davies sobbed. "She does not deserve this. She's innocent."

"I know," Mr. Davies said. "But she needs to know for her own safety."

Nell waited patiently for the pair to gather the confidence to inform her. She was terrified of what she may hear, but she had no idea she would be sickened by her own existence.

Davies informed her about her mother and who she was. And how her mother abandoned her at their doorsteps as a newborn barely two days old, with her name plastered throughout all of Britain's newspapers within a year. A name that everyone spits out after saying it. She will always go under this name.

She was grateful for Davies's naming her Nell, which allowed her to pretend she wasn't a prostitute's kid inside these four walls. She was simply another average lady within the orphanage, but now she had lost it as well. And the vultures waiting outside would attack on her the moment she took a foot out.

There have been far too many children arriving and departing from the orphanage, and some of them died while there, while others were unable to be helped. She was constantly heartbroken. But when Ethan died, something within her died too. It felt as if he were her own. And she will never have one; she will never be a mother, wife, or anything else.

Daviess were sorry they couldn't assist her anymore, but they had done so much for her, even when it caused nothing but troubles. The guilt in their eyes pained her.

The Daviess were the only people who cared about her. Mrs. Davies went so far as to beg Duchess for a job. She wasn't pleased, but she was grateful. But she knew she was alone. Nobody in their right mind would ever hire her.

The world was a horrible place if they were determined to sell a 15-year-old girl to a brothel for her parents' wickedness. She quickly knew it was the only location that would open her door if she ever found herself in such a situation. A boundary she never wanted to cross. It was kind of the Duchess to graciously decline Mrs. Davies. Even if Mrs. Davies was hoping the Duchess would accept her proposal, Nell was not. She was aware that she had run out of options.

She would have gone someplace else, changed her name and acquired a new identity. But she looked just like her mother, with the most distinctive pair of eyes and the most luxuriant golden hair, and she would draw undesired attention to herself. Everyone would soon find out. She had lived here her whole life and was not about to leave, only to discover that the creatures beyond her house were even worse than the demon on her doorstep. And they will search her down in every part of the planet. She felt protected here. It was her battlefield. She couldn't win, but she could hold her own.

The Duke's carriage came to a halt in front of the orphanage's door; Lady Donovan had come to see the Daviess and their children before departing for London. Donovan's had always contributed generously to the orphanage throughout the years, but Davies no longer had the strength to operate it, even if Donovan's paid for everything.

"Miss Nell, is it?" Lady Genevieve inquired after speaking with all the youngsters.

"Yes, my lady," Nell said calmly despite her nervousness. Mrs. Davies's remarks sparked an illogical hope in her that the Duchess would welcome her at her estate.

"Do you know my daughter, Lady Adelaide?" Lady Genevieve inquired.

"I know her, milady," she responded, "But I have never met her, milady"

"I believe she will be engaged soon," Lady Genevieve remarked with a grin. "I would like someone to run errands for me for everything that comes with the unification of two families, from engagement to wedding and much more. Do you want to work for me?"

"Yes," Nell said before her brain could understand what Lady Donovan had asked for. She just understood labour. She was too desperate to care at that point. Her whole existence was relieved at the possibility of postponing her certain death.

6

Chapter Six

Percival has been staying at Buckingham Palace since he arrived to London a week ago. He was accompanying a friend to prepare for the Prince's Ball, and parliament sessions were catching up with him.

The Kingdom was flourishing, and for the first time in generations, they had the most stable monarchy. While looking ahead to the future, his brother was quickly rising to become one of Britain's most prominent political personalities. However, rather than debating Kingdom plans, the Senate continued to drone on about the Crown Prince's marriage to a Spanish princess.

The Princess wasn't making things simpler for anybody. Percival, too, was facing her wrath for his friend's foolishness in keeping his lover in the castle after he had married the Princess. Everyone used to turn a blind eye to the royals and gentry's mistresses, but no one expected Princess to take it personally and make her husband's life miserable.

"You should tell her," Percival said.

"Tell whom? What?" The Crown Prince expressed confusion.

"The Princess," Percival said.

"If you haven't noticed, she doesn't let me speak," the prince said.

"Then just kiss her," Percival replied, causing Prince to splutter his wine.

"Why would I do that?" Prince expressed horror.

"To shut her up and declare your love for her," Percival said casually, as if they were discussing the weather.

"I do not love her," the Prince responded, horrified. "Why will I tell her something I don't mean?"

"Your Highness," Percival remarked mockingly, "Everyone around you observed how much you adore your wife. You aim to anger her because you like the attention she gives you after you've annoyed her. How much you enjoy seeing her flushed."

"Stop. Stop," Prince was quite flushed at his friend's blatant speech, "You are incorrect, as is everyone else. Did you forget how much I disliked marrying the foreign princess?"

"Yes, you did in the beginning," Percival responded, drinking his brandy. "However, your sentiments have altered with time. You love her. When she is in front of you, you find yourself unable to speak. Just accept it and tell her, and we'll all be saved from burning in your fire. It's unpleasant for all of us."

"I was against you getting married but now I seem to think a wife might bring your head in line," The Prince grumbled, "You are certainly losing it being delusional about me and the Princess."

"My buddy, do not be too late. Now, let's go check the ball preparation," Percival replied, putting a stop to the talk knowing full well that it would not go well.

When they reached the palace's huge ballroom, they were taken aback by how empty it was. The servants were removing some of the leftover decorations. After a succession of obscenities flung by the Prince, they discovered that the Princess had ordered the removal of all decorations.

While the Prince addressed his wife, which resulted in another of their squabbles, Percival stood quietly wishing that he would not get caught in the crossfire, but his wishes were answered when the Princess approached and stood in front of him, with his buddy at her heels.

"Senor," the Princess said with a heavy Spanish accent.

"Your Highness," Percival bowed politely.

"Tell me, am I not the daughter in law of this Kingdom and the future queen?" She inquired, hands on her hips and a scowling expression on her face.

"You are, your highness," Percival said without hesitation.

"Did I not come here leaving my home and everything I know to marry your idiota prince?" She inquired haughtily.

"You did, your highness," Percival remarked, amused by his friend's horrified reaction as Princess referred to the future king as a fool.

"Is it wrong for me to create some semblance of home here through the ball?" She inquired, her voice low and hurtful as it coated her cheeks.

Percival glanced over to his pal, who had noticed the same thing! The Princess missed her home.

"Do you want the ball to be Spanish style, your highness?" he questioned the distressed princess.

"Yes," she said, her face lighting up like a Christmas tree. She came to the notion that despised her and married the prince at an age when she should have been enjoying balls and having fun. Percival's adoration for the princess grew to new heights.

"Then we shall have it that way," Percival remarked, telling the Princess, "I am sure the Queen and King will allow it for their favourite daughter-in-law."

"I am their only daughter-in-law," she replied, sulking.

"Well, then they don't have a choice, do they?" He remarked, making Princess grin.

"I will not allow it," The Prince said, "Not everyone is pleased with our marriage. I do not want to irritate them anymore."

"Maybe it's time they know who saved them from their own destruction," he told his companion, smiling at Princess. "It's time everyone accepts their future queen."

"It is not a good idea, Percival," Prince said. "The parliament session will be outraged on hearing this."

"Then we shall keep it a secret till the last moment," Percival remarked with a sneer. "Your Highness, I will send a call to you as soon as I get an audience with the King and Queen to discuss the plans for the ball."

"You are my friend; you should be on my side," the Prince replied, crossing after the Princess had departed.

"Well, my dear friend, I am on your side," Percival remarked, winking. "A happy wife means a happy life. She is correct: you are an idiot if you haven't recognized it yet."

"It is going to be outrageous, a Spanish ball on British land," The Prince looked terrified, "I can already hear people murmuring."

"We will find something more outrageous for people to talk about," Percival promised his pal. "It won't be that bad."

"How will it even be ready on time? She's scraped the entire ballroom," the Prince protested.

"Then we better help her with everything we have," he remarked, marching towards the castle.

When Percival took full responsibility for assisting the Princess in her preparation, the King and Queen were readily persuaded. Percival hoped his buddy would come to his senses and heal the rift between him and his wife.

The Parliament session was scheduled to be divided into two halves. One finishes a month from now, while the other begins after two weeks of Christmas break and lasts a month before ending for the year. The Prince's Ball will be held at the completion of Parliament, giving them two and a half months to prepare.

Percival was relishing the ball preparation for the first time in his life. He has been following his buddy the prince since he was 21, and they have always preferred parliament sessions over dances and soirees. But, as Prince's buddy, he couldn't actively participate in politics, and he couldn't abandon his friend.

When Cedric joined politics, Percival stood aside to allow his younger brother to follow his goal while he fulfilled his duties as Whitworth's heir, controlling all Whitworth investments and banks while preparing to join the Crown Prince's privy council.

The royal family looked up to the Whitworths as friends and trusted advisers, and it was Whitworth's responsibility to preside over the privy Council. Whitworth has traditionally been the royal family's extended hands, carrying out numerous jobs for the monarchy while also keeping the British economy afloat with their affluent banks, allowing the Kingdom to thrive.

Percival knew his father was becoming old and wanted nothing more than to pass everything on to his children and spend the rest of the day with his mother, so he was more than willing to take over as Whitworth's head. With a woman at his side, he would be in an ideal position to succeed as the future heir of Whitworth. And, with Addie's letter approving his courtship proposal, he was prepared to propose to her on Christmas Eve.

7

Chapter Seven

She was destitute of everything, with men around her and ready to assault. She was soaked in perspiration, her pulse thumping in her chest as she tried valiantly to concentrate on her surroundings. The mocking laughter sounded in her ears. The eyes looked at her in the same way that a predator would stare at its victim. They were closing in on her, making it harder for her to move. Nell awoke shocked and bewildered from the nightmare, completely afraid.

She'd never experienced such horror before. Rocking back and forth in an attempt to calm herself, she glanced around to assure she was secure within Donovan Manor and that the nightmare was not real.

She has been working at Donovan Manor since Davies's departure for London. Her first day was difficult; for the first time, she had to deal with the other servant residing within the manor's constant contempt and mocking. She was relieved that no one attempted to physically hurt her, since everyone despised her.

When a number of staff protested to the Duke that she shouldn't continue at the manor, the Duchess denied their objection, pushing them to give her a chance while warning her not to do anything that would endanger their reputation.

Everyone returned to ignoring her after that. She was given a cot in a storage area where wood and hay were kept. She worked carefully and without error, pleased that everyone ignored her save for the odd nasty glance. Lady Genevieve quickly noted Nell's hard work and dedication, and her ability to complete every duty assigned to her while making no errors earned her favor with the Duchess.

Despite everyone's objections and Addie's recommendation, she made Nell her companion after three weeks of being at Donovan Manor and assigned her a servant's quarter.

She continued to get up before daybreak even when Lady Genevieve did not need her till after breakfast was served. She assisted the servants with their work only with their permission, hoping to obtain their praise. Lady Genevieve created her companion to restrict her relationship with others and maintain control over everything concerning Nell, but Nell wanted others to treat her as if she were just another person.

Lady Genevieve was seldom without Lady Seraphina, and Nell came to admire both women more and more. She admired both of the women and listened intently to everything they said. She was astounded by the two ladies' acceptance of her. Lady Adelaide was also kind to her and tried to become her friend, but Nell knew better than to get close to anybody.

Every day, Lady Genevieve and Lady Seraphina would gush over their children's prospective weddings. Nell couldn't help but love the ladies' excitement. She was just a spectator, but she couldn't help but wish Lady Adelaide a great future as Lady Whitworth.

Even although she was never a member of society and remained in the shadows, she understood Lady Addie's desire for marriage. This might be her final season to find a good spouse. The world was unkind to everyone, rich and poor; some had the resources to hide, some to fight, and others were left exposed to spite.

Everyone was constantly talking about the Whitworths, and although she had never seen him, she had heard a lot about Lord Percival Whitworth and felt he would make an excellent spouse for Lady Addie. She struggled to resist pity from pouring into her. She would have no idea what a good or horrible spouse is.

Nell was loading her valises, triple-checking the list of everything Duchess had ordered from London for the Christmas event. Instead of Christmas Eve, both women were preparing for an engagement party. Despite Lady Addie's protests that Lord Percival and she haven't settled on anything yet and that they shouldn't get ahead of themselves with the celebrations, the women insisted she will marry this season.

Nell quickly understood how oblivious the women were of Lady Addie's situation, and she felt horrible about running away every time Lady Addie sought to befriend her. Despite being a beloved part of Donovan's family, she felt Lady Addie was lost and more alone with each passing day, but she could do nothing. If someone other than Whitworth had married Lady Addie, her sheer presence would have sparked a mutiny.

She arrived in London at lunchtime and experienced freedom for the first time in her life. She worked only for Donovan as a maid. Everything seemed like a fairytale. She was smiling uncontrollably, with no criticism from anybody. The butler looked at her strangely, but he didn't comprehend her delight. The desire to flee into the streets and vanish forever was strong in her.

Then she recalled the lady's compassion, which allowed her to be here. She accompanied the butler inside, where she was led to her room for the duration of her stay and served lunch. She was on Lord Percival Whitworth's private estate, but there were very few people there. It seemed more like an abandoned mansion than the residence of Prince's closest friend. She only met the butler and chef, Mr. and Mrs. Fitzgerald, who were well into their fifties.

She wanted to explore the estate and go outdoors to see the world. She didn't know when she'd come back, but she kept herself from succumbing to temptation. After recovering for the day, she joined the rest of the group for supper. Along with the chef and butler, there were two ladies, Sophia and Eleanor, who helped clean and maintain the estate, two additional men who came to assist in the morning, and two guards for protection.

She discovered that his lordship no longer lives on this estate; instead, he is either in Whitworth manor or at Royal Palace with the Prince, where he is now residing. The talk with all of the ladies came smoothly; chatting to others without hesitation about her was incredible. She wanted to cry with excitement. Everyone soon retired, and the two maids spoke to her till midnight, their joy rubbing off on her.

She awoke as usual at the crack of dawn and was unable to go back asleep. She moved toward the kitchen to check if anybody had awoken. Her heart sank as she heard shuffling from the direction of the front entrance, the sound of someone attempting to open the door sounding like a drum in an otherwise quiet house. Taking deep breaths, she headed toward the door after retrieving a frying pan from the kitchen.

As she stood with her weapon in the air, waiting for the intruder to smash through the door, the other side became quiet, and there were two hard bangs on the door. Her thoughts raced, and she figured the guy on the other end must be one of the two men that arrive in the morning to assist out.

She gingerly stepped forward, grasping the pan securely in one hand and slowly opened the door with the other. As she narrowed her eyes to see the person standing in front of her, he collapsed, throwing all of his weight on her and unbalancing her, the pan dropping from her grasp with a loud clang while her arms wrapped around him to balance.

The guy in her arms seems to be losing consciousness as his arms wrap around her waist, hugging her securely and placing his head on her shoulder, breathing deeply.

"My Lord," she heard Mr. Fitzgerald say as he approached them along the hallway.

Her eyes widened to the size of a saucer when she realized the person in her arms was the estate's lord, Lord Percival Whitworth, and that he was blazing like a fire.

8

Chapter Eight

Percival felt as if his body was being punctured with frigid needles. It was a marvel he made it back to his estate alive, despite having what seemed to be a high temperature. He was going to be really ill, and the princess was going to kill him for leaving her in the midst of ball preparations. However, if he was to recover from his condition, he needed to leave the Royal Residence and return to his estate.

He attempted unsuccessfully to open the front door; his body was freezing and he was trying to remain awake. He subsequently regretted leaving the Royal Residence with a stolen royal Arabian mare without informing anybody.

He pounded on the door, hoping Mr. Fitzgerald would hear him and come to search for him, laying half-conscious on the threshold. He was being silly, but he couldn't remain at the royal while he was unwell and the word of the princess falling for him spread through the royal hallways.

The door opened unexpectedly, his already weakening senses unable to hold him erect. Before he knew it, he was colliding with a warm and soft body. His frigid senses found warmth in the heated flesh that touched him. He wrapped his arms around a slender waist, filling his lungs with a distinct relaxing odor.

He wobbled to his bedchamber with the assistance of his butler and an unknown person, while Mrs. Fitzgerald made herbal tea and sent one of the guards for the doctor. Nell ran to the kitchen, grabbed cold water, and began laying a washcloth on his forehead to chill him down until the doctor came.

Percival felt as if his whole existence was buried in ice, and the chill on his forehead was caused by Satan himself. He was exhausted and shivering from the extreme cold. He was battling to prevent himself from falling into oblivion.

He awoke as someone pushed a horrible drink down his neck. He recognized Mr. Fitzgerald's and his doctor's voices, as well as the presence of someone with a haunting voice that soothed his mind. He was worried about being delirious.

Percival continued falling in and out of awareness; he would awaken when someone attempted to force-feed him medication or food, only to fall back into darkness again. He lost track of time, but he was always aware of who was taking care of him. He would have recognized if it was his butler or chef. He had never met any of the service staff engaged at his estate, but he wished he knew the guy who looked after him. Percival wanted to celebrate the loving nature.

He awoke feeling much better and hungry. The fire was blazing in the hearth, and the darkness surrounding him suggested that he had awoken in the middle of the night. The disease has made him frail, and he can hardly get out of bed. He saw movement in the corner of his room and couldn't believe his luck; an intruder had opted to break in when he could barely stand upright. He should have listened to his brothers who begged him to employ extra assistance for his land.

Before he could respond, the intruder saw him standing near his bed, and the figure began creeping towards him in the darkness. He collected all of his remaining power; he'd be damned if he didn't battle as long as his feeble body allowed.

"My Lord," he heard the figure say in a beautiful tone.

As the figure emerged from the shadows, it transformed into a stunning lady, capturing his whole attention. She was very lovely. Her beautiful golden blonde hair, fair complexion, and blue eyes mesmerized him.

He'd never seen a more lovely lady. He never wanted to leave the lovely dream.

"My Lord," she whispered in an appealing whisper, "you shouldn't be standing."

He was locked in place, a victim of Medusa's stare. A voice in his brain screamed that he was hallucinating, but a bigger part of him wanted it to be true.

His concentration was completely concentrated on the lady in his room; he didn't notice when his butler arrived and stood close him, attempting to get his attention.

"My Lord," Mr. Fitzgerald murmured, guiding Percival back to his bed. "I will send for the doctor right now. Miss Nell, will you kindly take after his lordship's needs?"

The woman nodded and approached him as if he were a dream that would disappear in an instant. Percival couldn't believe his fantasy wasn't a dream and that the lady standing in front of him was real.

"My lord, you should lay down. I'll ask Mrs. Fitzgerald to prepare something for you," she said, and he finally recognized the voice he'd been hearing.

After placing him back into bed, she exited his rooms to get his chef. When he was alone with just his thoughts and a growling tummy, the truth became clearer. She seemed familiar, but he couldn't recall where he'd met her; he was certain she wasn't working at his estate.

He didn't know the service people in his employment, like any other gentry, but when he relieved all of his staff and entrusted Mr. and Mrs. Fitzgerald to run his estate in his absence, the only female help that remained were two young sisters who were as close to the Fitzgeralds as their daughters. However, the lady had a remarkable look that was unlike any of the sisters.

Instead of her, Mrs. Fitzgerald entered his bedchamber with the food on her plate.

"Mrs. Fitzgerald, how are you?" He inquired; his voice barely audible.

"My lord, I am completely well, but you are not. I made your favorite soup, and the doctor will be here soon," she replied, delicately setting the meal on his bed.

"Mrs. Fitzgerald, who was the woman that was in my bed-chamber before?" He asked.

"My lord, her name is Nell. She is a maid on Donovan's estate who came here to do Lady Whitworth and Lady Donovan's errands. She was the one who discovered you at the door and has been caring for you ever since. She is such a sweet girl," Mrs. Fitzgerald said.

Percival recognized why she seemed familiar. But why didn't he see such a lovely face at the Donovan estate? He requested Mrs. Fitzgerald to send

Nell to his bedchamber. After waiting for many seconds with his soup becoming colder and no intention of drinking, he was disappointed when his door opened to see Dr. Alexander and his butler, but no indication of her.

Following a few inquiries from his doctor and a thorough examination, he was recommended bed rest for a week and plenty of liquid meals. Doctor Alexander left and instructed his butler to deliver Nell to his bedchamber. Mr. Fitzgerald promised to bring him hot soup while removing the untouched one from his side.

While he waited for her, he felt his energies slip away. He heard two knocks on his door, and she appeared in front of him once again. He stared at her attentively as she arranged the meal appropriately. There was a sense of maturity that comes with age, yet her curious attitude indicated she had a sheltered existence and a natural resistance.

"Miss Hawthorne," he shouted.

9

Chapter Nine

"Miss Hawthorne."

Her delighted bubble shattered and dissipated in thin air. Her fantasy came crashing down on her.

"Yes, milord," she said, trying not to let her voice crack.

The stillness stretched between them, and Nell couldn't stop herself from gazing up. His black eyes were bewildered and fixed on her, and she could not see the end of those dark pools.

"The soup," she blurted out without thinking. "The soup is getting cold, milord."

Her remarks jolted Percival out of his stupor, and as he attempted to pick up the scoop of soup, a strong wave of nausea washed over him.

"I do not feel the strength in my arms," he remarked, attempting to concentrate his eyesight.

"You've been sleeping for three days, milord, without food," she added, assisting him with water.

"Three days!!" he cried.

"Yes, milord," she said, holding a scoop of soup to serve him.

He ate silently as she fed him, without looking into his eyes.

"Felix wrote to me that Aunt Genevieve gave you a job at her estate; I hope you enjoy Donovan's," he remarked, attempting to strike up a discussion.

"I am, milord, and Lady Donovan is very kind," she said, her eyes downcast.

"I hope you received all of Mr. Fitzgerald's assistance with your visit to London," he remarked after a little pause.

"Yes, milord, Mr. and Mrs. Fitzgerald have been very helpful," she responded.

"Miss Hawthorne,"

"Nell," she snapped.

They both froze when they heard her strong reaction. Nell regained her composure before they realized she had humiliated the Lord of the Manor.

"I am sorry, milord; I will go immediately." She began apologizing loudly. She turned suddenly to go.

"Nell," He whispered quietly, and she felt a weight in her gut as he spoke her name. The sensation was unfamiliar and frightening.

"Nell," he called her again, and she veiled her face to seem emotionless before turning back to him as the butterflies in her stomach continued to cause havoc.

"I am sorry, milord; I should not have spoken to you in such a manner," she apologized again.

"You do not like to be called by your mother's name," he said.

She'd never felt more vulnerable as she did in front of him. He didn't have the strength to rise up, while she was on the edge of dropping down.

"Yes, milord," she said, her voice breaking.

"I understand, please forgive me if I have caused you any distress," he replied.

She wanted him to stop talking; his words reminded her of all she had forgotten in the previous several days.

"Milord, I should go. The doctor prescribed a lot of rest for you to get well," she remarked, scooping up the lunch dish and leaving.

"Mrs. Fitzgerald told me you were the one that took care of me while I was unconscious," he continued, not wanting her to depart so quickly.

"Everyone was busy with their chores, and I was the only one who could spare the time," she answered in a clipped tone, irritated at him for making her feel so vulnerable.

He laughed aloud at her candid remarks.

"I will bring some of the help back to the estate," he chuckled.

Nell looked up at him for the first time since entering his room. He assumed she criticized him, but instead of being disrespectful, he laughed. His chuckle made her grin. He looked captivating in the night light, smiling with tears in the corners of his eyes. She was witnessing Lord Percival Whitworth, as recounted in the Gazette, and the ladies fawning over him. She diverted her gaze before he saw her looking at him.

"Thank you for taking care of me, Miss Nell," he expressed gratitude.

"Good night, milord," she replied, leaving his room perplexed.

By the time she got to bed, she was overcome with anxiety and concern. She was pacifying herself by recalling her days of independence. She was certain he knew about her history, and that everyone in the mansion would soon find out, bringing disdain and loathing her way once again.

As exchange for caring for him, she intended to insist that he maintain her secret until she arrived in London, where she could enjoy the fresh air before returning to her claustrophobic existence.

She couldn't sleep all night, tossing and turning, not wanting daybreak to arrive. She couldn't stop worrying about what might happen the next day. She never expected him to realize she cared for him when he was unwell. Once he recovered, he was going to be furious that a lowlife like her was ever near him.

When the daylight arrived, she accepted her destiny. She awoke and prepared to do all of her tasks as fast as possible so she could return. Her tasks would have been accomplished if Lady Whitworth hadn't written to urge her to postpone everything and assist the Fitzgeralds in caring for her son, despite the fact that there was very little support available on his estate.

She was perplexed; as a Whitworth, she couldn't understand why he released so many of his troops when he clearly could afford it. Pushing all thoughts to the back of her mind, she concentrated on doing all of the errands.

She alerted Mr. Fitzgerald of the conveyance and, at Mrs. Fitzgerald's request, prepared to depart after breakfast before being summoned to his lordship again. She could no longer face him; every time she saw Percival Whitworth, she felt nervous. His friendliness unnerved her. He was, after all, a gentleman, and she could never be certain of his motives. And now that he was aware of her background, she should be extra cautious with others.

She stepped out towards the carriage, making sure she had given the driver the correct directions. She left the estate but couldn't do anything. She arrived later than her appointment since she couldn't leave while Percival was still sick. Everyone pledged to complete all assignments before the end of the week. She was thinking about how to avoid everyone back on the estate as she returned fatigued from walking across London's streets. By now, his lordship must have informed Mr. and Mrs. Fitzgerald about her, and all she could do was stay out of everyone's business.

To her astonishment, nothing about the estate had changed. Everyone was still nice and kind to her. The most difficult thing for her was avoiding Percival. In a day, he was out of bed and walking about his estate, while everyone else was unable to request that he rest. Everyone went to her to help his lord relax. She disregarded everyone's plaintive gaze, hoping to make Percival see reason.

A day later, she was on her way to ensure that everything was on track and she could depart by the end of the week. As she waited for the carriage to leave the estate after ordering the driver, she heard the door open and Percival sat in front of her, knocking for the carriage to depart.

"A fly might get in your mouth, Miss Nell," He chuckled, causing her lips to close.

"What are you doing, milord?" She inquired when the immediate amazement subsided.

"I was losing my mind cooped up in the estate, so I thought I will get some fresh air," he remarked with a laugh.

"Cooped up! You should have been sleeping, but you were wandering about the estate, not exactly cozied up," she added, folding her hands in front of her, making him giggle.

"You are funny, Miss Nell," he replied, giggling.

"If I had known you needed fresh air, I would have taken a different carriage, milord," she responded furiously, blaming him for derailing her intentions to avoid him.

"There is no other carriage available on the estate, Miss Nell," He replied teasingly. "I will have to send the letter to the Prince to send my carriage back and I do not want him to summon me back to court just yet."

"I believe Whitworth's have more than enough carriages for each family member," she stated with a smile.

"They do. But I wanted to join you on your errands, Miss Nell, and I hope my presence is not unpleasant." He smiled.

She couldn't possibly toss him out of his carriage when he was still healing. She wanted to chastise him like a kid and confine him in his bedchamber. But he was a Lord, and she shouldn't be seated in front of him. She had no option but to let him do what he wanted.

"So, what is the first thing on our list?" He asked sincerely.

"Milord," she said, perplexed.

"I came to know you couldn't complete your errands since you were taking care of me while I was ill, I would like to help you with them," he offered earnestly.

He laughed again when he saw her puzzled expression.

10

Chapter Ten

Percival felt Nell looked really stunning pouting. She was upset with him, so he wanted to tease her even more. He did not know her, yet he was drawn to her like a moth to a flame. Despite her numerous challenges in life, she emanated strength and none of the shortcomings.

He wanted to know whether she was another person or if she was frigid to the bone. He continued to examine her as she stared out the window. A curl of her golden hair fell on her wonderfully curved neck, eliciting savage sensations inside him. He gulped consciously.

"So, what is the first thing on our list?" He inquired, careful to project a serious tone.

"Milord," she said, perplexed.

"I came to know you couldn't complete your errands since you were taking care of me while I was ill, I would like to help you with them," he offered earnestly.

Her bewildered expression made him giggle once more. He couldn't imagine that just observing someone could bring him such delight. She was absolutely intriguing.

When his laughing stopped, he discovered she was staring at him. He realized he may not be as welcome as he imagined. Every woman he had come into contact with since the season began was batting her lashes at him in an attempt to impress him, and he had never seen any woman glare at him like the one in front of him was doing right now.

He was conscious of the impact he had on the ladies, even though he did not live his life like Tavi or Dom. However, the lady in front of him seemed impervious to him, which was extremely pleasant. She did not view him as anything more than a bother.

"Have you ever been to London before?" He asked.

"No," she said curtly.

"Didn't the Daviess shift to London and moved all the children to the orphanage here?" He inquired cautiously, analyzing her response. Her expression relaxes dramatically, and her tongue moves to moisten her lips.

"Yes," she muttered. "I don't know their address or the name of the orphanage."

The wheels in his head began to turn, wondering why the folks who looked after her wouldn't disclose her their address. Before he could say anything, she spoke up.

"I never thought I'd come to London in this lifetime," she remarked, her expression emotionless, "It was pointless for me to know where the Daviess lived."

"Why did you think you will never come to London, Miss Nell?" He inquired carefully.

"I never considered leaving the orphanage; it was my home, my safe haven," she smiled, recalling the past.

"So, you never wished to visit London, which part of Great Britain did you wish to visit?" He asked.

"None," she said.

There was no regret in her comments, just certainty; she had accepted the hand destiny gave her. Her cheerful surrender to life worried him. He wanted her to see and experience the outside world.

"Well, now that you're in London, which location do you want to see first? London Tower? Hyde Garden? What about the Thames? The palace?" He inquired enthusiastically.

"I want to finish the errands and return to Donovan's estate, milord," she remarked with a glint in her eye. She was no longer staring or irritated at him. She was just as mischievous as he was, but she wasn't kidding when she stated she wanted to come back.

The remainder of the voyage was spent in quiet. He followed her around while she accomplished all of her prescribed duties. Thanks to his plain clothing and large hat, no one recognized him, and he was able to spend a day with troops.

Despite living in the same location and breathing the same air, people's lifestyles differed significantly. The distinction between classes is clearly obvious. Never before had he stepped outside of his comfort zone to see the lives of others who made things easy for them.

He was fascinated by the simplicity of the people, picturing how his life would have been if he hadn't been the heir to Whitworth. He might have become a lawyer battling for justice in court, returning home to a modest cottage with his wife waiting for him, and all his exhaustion would evaporate with a glance at her. He imagined Nell, the lady who was presently criticizing the shop owner, as his wife.

It was a wonderful fantasy that will never come true. He is and will always be the heir to Whitworth, one day succeeding his father and propelling the Whitworth name to new heights, married to the lady he does not love but hopes to one day.

"Today's chores are finished, milord; we'll return to the estate now," Nell replied, glancing up at the lord, who was buried in his thoughts.

"Milord," she whispered, prodding at his elbow to get him out of his thoughts.

"Yes," he responded. "Please be seated I will be inside in a moment."

"Is everything alright, milord?" She inquired worriedly. He had been out of sorts since they went to the first shop. She's enjoyed his jokes, but she's also observed him thinking deeply. She was surprised that she loved his company when she anticipated him to annoy her.

She was surprised by how quickly the carriage came to a halt. She peered out the window and realized they weren't on the estate, but rather in front of a massive park.

"Ah, we are here," Percival remarked, stepping out of the carriage as soon as they arrived.

He extended his hand to Nell, who gazed at him as if he were from another species.

"My Lady," he began like a gentleman, "would you please step out of the carriage?"

"No," she said.

Percival remained there, wondering what had occurred, as she glanced the other way, folding her arms in front of her, sulking. Percival sat in front of her once again, trying not to chuckle.

"What's the problem, my lady?" He said, adopting a similar position as her.

"I am not a lady," she snapped.

"Miss Nell, what is wrong?" He inquired again, gently.

"Nothing, milord," she responded. "I will stay inside the carriage till you run your errands and we can be on our way back to the estate."

"My errand requires you," he said, pausing to see her horrified expression.

"Why?" She squeaked.

Percival was quickly alerted to the fact that something terrible had occurred to her. Her anxiety of leaving her home, as well as her reluctance to travel new areas, stemmed from something in her past.

"This is Hyde Park, Miss Nell," he said calmly. "One of London's royal parks. All of the royal homes, including Buckingham Palace, Kensington Palace and Gardens, and several royal dwellings, are located along its borders. It is available to everybody, nobles and commoners alike. This is where the regular people get closest to monarchy."

"Why are you telling me this?" She asked cautiously.

"There is a little cream ice store at the end of the route that serves the best cream ice in all of London. It was superior to the cream ice made by royal cooks. Would you want to join me there? I promise it will be worthwhile," he remarked, smiling frankly.

He had no idea what she was looking for on his face, but it seems she found it when she answered yes.

They were soon going down the gravel road, the red of the setting sun lighting up everything around them. After paying for the cream ice, Percival intended to wait beneath the tree and watch the sunset, but recognizing she wouldn't return, he took her on a tour for as long as he could.

She quickly understood he was eating his cream ice slowly in order to spend more time touring with her, and with each passing minute, an unfamiliar sensation began to settle in her.

11

Chapter Eleven

The following several days, Percival continued nagging Nell, accompanying her on errands, and she made sure to extend everything until sunset so he wouldn't take her to any more sightseeing. Percival was lively and pleasant, never crossing his boundary. He always took his position as a Lord, exuding a sense of regality.

Nell was having difficulty maintaining indifferent and stoic faces while being entertained by everything around her. Percival was the only one who seemed unconcerned with her background after Lady Addie, treating her as if she were any other regular person. And her frigid walls were beginning to thaw.

After three days of rushing about London, she had done all of her tasks, and the shipments were on their way to Donovan's. She was going to miss Lord Percival's presence, which annoyed her. He has been present around her in some capacity from the day she came. And today was her reprieve before departing for Donovan in two days. She planned to spend the remainder of her time with Mrs. Fitzgerald, Sophia, and Eleanor, all of whom had become her friends in recent days.

"Nell," Sophia said, banging on the door.

"Sophia, come inside," she urged, opening the door. "I was coming to you. Today is my free day, and I wanted to spend it with you and Eleanor before heading to Donovan's."

"His Lordship has asked you to get ready and meet him outside," Sophia said with a worried expression on her face. "I thought all your errands were over, we were looking forward to spending time with you, Nell."

"My errands are over," she remarked, perplexed. "Do you know why His Lordship ask for me?" Sophia, still agitated, continued, "He also asked to prepare the carriage; I believe you must accompany him."

"Where is His Lordship? I will talk with him; I am sure he does not want me to join him," she reassured Sophia. She was on her way to his bedchamber when Mr. Fitzgerald stopped her.

"Miss Nell, what are you still doing here?" He inquired, "Didn't Sophia notify you of his Lordship's request?"

"Yes, she did. I..."

"So, what are you doing here? His Lordship is waiting for you outside in his carriage," he replied with displeasure. She made it to the carriage outside in no time.

"Milord," she whispered, gazing into the carriage, where Percival's face was hidden beneath the ledger.

"Ah, Miss Nell, you're here; please come inside," he said, beaming his most attractive grin.

"What is this about?" She inquired skeptically.

"Please step inside the carriage, Miss Nell, and I will answer all of your questions," he added, hiding behind the Gazette once again.

Nell could not believe he was behaving like a kid.

"Milord," she said, but he did not respond.

She continued to remain, her fury building as she watched the carriage driver standing uncomfortably. She wanted to burst back into his mansion. She did not have the right to disrespect the Lord of the manor.

She sat in front of him, enraged, and did not attempt to soothe him. A second later, the carriage began to move, and he was still hiding behind the Gazette, stirring her rage even more.

Without thinking, she pulled the copy of Gazette from him, showing his beaming face as she realized what he was doing.

"Miss Nell," he said happily.

"I do not appreciate your games, milord," she said sincerely.

"I assure you that I am not playing any games, Miss Nell," he said with similar seriousness.

She was unhappy, and instead of responding, she sat quietly staring out the carriage window. She didn't like how she was responding to him by letting him do anything he wanted. She kept reminding herself that he was the master of the manor and that defying his orders would be foolish, but it was just an excuse to explain her motives for being in his company. They traveled in solitude, thinking about each other.

"We are here," he said as the carriage drew to a standstill.

He got out of the carriage and extended his hand to her. When she gazed out, her steps paused in response to what she saw. Percival was closely observing her; her lovely blue eyes were filled with tears, and her smile captivated him. She wandered in a stupor towards the door of the orphanage, where the Daviess were waiting for her.

"Nell, my child," Mrs. Davies hugged her fiercely, crying into her shoulder.

After a tearful reunion, they entered the orphanage to see the children who had yet to be adopted. Nell was surrounded by youngsters, some of whom she had previously cared for in an orphanage; the others followed suit and joined her.

Soon, she was handed a package full of candy and chocolates, and she glanced up to find Percival beaming at her.

"I thought you'd want to bring something for the kids; there are also toys," he remarked, moving on to another set of kids.

He made it difficult for people to stop appreciating him. She saw nothing wrong with admiring the guy in front of her, who was sitting on the dirty floor, presenting presents to every kid and listening closely. But the strange sensation that crept within her every time he smiled or looked at her was becoming more frightening.

Their gazes met above the group of youngsters around them, and among all the people and sounds, their grins for each were the brightest. The smiles on both of their faces lasted till the conclusion of the day, as they enjoyed themselves with everyone.

"You are happy," Mrs. Davies observed, sitting alongside her as Percival handed the meal to the children.

"It is fine to admit you are happy, just as long as you admit you have the worst life on the planet," Mrs. Davies said, chuckling.

"What's the purpose if it's gone soon? And I'll return to my dark place," she murmured.

"Nothing remains forever, Nell," Mrs. Davies remarked. "You learn to embrace the happy in the time rather than worrying about the grief that will come. And when the grief comes, you must brace your heart and faith that it will pass."

Nell didn't say anything since she had nothing to say.

"He is different, isn't he?" Mrs. Davies inquired, seeing Percival.

"Very much so," she said.

"And he put efforts to make you happy, doesn't he?" Mrs. Davies inquired.

"He shouldn't have," she said abruptly.

"It is a pity he is a Lord," she remarked. "It is even sadder that society is cruel enough to keep people away from the one that can make them happy."

"He also irritates, annoys, and angers me," Nell replied with a grimace.

Mrs. Davies laughed aloud at her remarks.

"Isn't that perfect?" She inquired once her laughing had faded.

"I do not understand what you are talking about," Nell replied as she walked away.

"Ignorance is not bliss, my daughter," Mrs. Davies said.

As evening fell, the adults struggled to keep up with the enthusiasm of youngsters. Mr. Davies appeared shortly after, insisting that Nell talk with him directly.

"It's good to see you healthy and doing well, Nell," he replied, offering her a glass of wine.

"Thank you, Mr. Davies," she responded. "How is your health?"

"Deteriorating, I would be lucky if I could see next winter," he remarked.

He seemed unwell and weary. Nell never had a connection with Mr. Davies, but he was the closest father figure she had in her life, and seeing him slowly die made her sad.

"You should know better than to get close to a Lord," He added after a little quiet.

"I am not close to any Lord, Mr. Davies," she said coldly.

"I think it is my responsibility to warn you once," he said.

"And if it has been said, then I will take your leave," she added, standing up and walking away without looking back.

After an emotional goodbye, Nell and Percival returned to the estate. Percival didn't say anything till they entered the mansion. Something in her demeanor altered following the conversation with Mr. Davies, and he decided it was best to let her deal with it.

"Good night, Miss Nell," he replied, standing on the steps leading to his room and walked away without waiting for her response.

"Milord," she said out. Percival looked back, waiting for her to speak.

"Thank you," she replied, looking away from him.

Percival went away after telling her good night once again, and she remained there staring at his disappearing back.

"I am, in this very moment, happy," she told herself.

12

Chapter Twelve

Percival entered his room, unable to keep a grin off his face. He was ecstatic because he had gotten a letter from his private investigator, who had identified the Daviess' residence and the orphanage where they were staying within a day. It was tough for him to keep the knowledge to himself while yet surprising Nell at the appropriate moment. He couldn't wait for the normally cold and stoic lady, who was generally upset with him, to lose her cool.

He was overjoyed when Nell froze at the sight of his surprise. Her tears disturbed him, but the euphoria that followed them filled him with pride. He cherished every minute at the orphanage, surprised by the children's fortitude and how they found delight in the slightest of things, whilst the wealthy moan over little details. And his regard for Nell grew more with each passing second; after all, she was one of them.

His eyes constantly revealed his thoughts, searching for her wherever she went, and when she smiled, he saw paradise. She might put the goddess of beauty to shame. He felt fascinated, as if a mortal had submitted to the goddess' gaze. He was aware that Mrs. Davies and Nell were staring at him and chatting about him. He could feel her eyes on him, making it impossible to restrain him from marching towards her and drowning in her blue stare.

For the following two days, he was occupied being punished by the Princess. When he faced the anger of the prince and princess, his plan to accompany Nell to Donovan's went out the window. His butler told him that she was going tomorrow, and despite the princess's threat to murder him if he left the palace, he returned to his estate to say goodbye before she departed. He wondered if he could invite Nell to remain so he could tour her about London and spend more time with her.

"My Lord," Mr. Fitzgerald knocked on his door, carrying his favorite brandy.

"Lady Whitworth sent another letter from the Donovan's, my Lord," Mr. Fitzgerald remarked, giving him the glass.

"What does it say?" He inquired, sitting in front of the fire.

"My Lord, the party will be in London in two days for the season, and I would want you to be present at the Whitworth Manor. Lady Whitworth has also requested you to contact your brothers," his butler said.

"Who all are coming?" He asked casually.

"Lord and Lady Donovan, and Lady Adelaide, my Lord."

"Thank you, Mr. Fitzgerald," he said. "Is Miss Nell all set to leave?"

"No, my Lord. Lady Whitworth has requested Miss Nell to be Lady Adelaide's handmaid and to be there at Whitworth Manor when they arrive, thus she is not allowed to leave London."

He had a sense of dread; the lady he was intended to marry and the woman he was drawn to live under the same roof, which disturbed him. When Nell returned from her conversation with Mr. Davies, her face was paler and more stiff than normal, and she was filled with rage.

He was so preoccupied with Nell that he forgot about Adelaide. He felt like a jerk; he had given hope to one innocent lady and was now becoming involved with another. He was so overjoyed when she showed her thanks in two words, "thank you," that he forgot the larger promise of marriage to another.

He was aware of his potential from a young age; being the heir to the Duchy of Whitworth, he was treated differently than his brothers, almost like royalty. And he never wanted to be anything other than what everyone expected of him.

He always admired his parents and wished for a relationship similar to theirs. For years, he had hoped to meet someone he could love and who would love him back. But he quickly understood that love, like his parents', was not for everyone and was almost impossible, since everyone desired nothing more than to acquire his favor.

He had given up hope and accepted his destiny of loveless marriage, and the season only strengthened his decision to end it as soon as possible, and in his hurry, he led an innocent creature whose future now rests on his shoulders. And just when he believed it was over, he glanced up and saw what he had been looking for all his life, so close but out of grasp.

Nell was undeniably gorgeous, but more than that, he adored the way she made him feel. Her contempt for his rank made him feel liberated. She tries so hard to remain linked to the chain she constructed for herself, but she was a free spirit by nature, and with her, he might break free from the shackles of the society that trapped him.

He would have been the happiest person in the world if he could make her his, but he had always prioritized his role as an heir to the Duchy of Whitworth above anything else, and he was not about to alter that now. He will spend a life bound by duty with a lady he can't imagine loving anymore, his family proud of him, and his relationship with the future King unblemished.

The following day, Percival left instructions for the party's preparation with Whitworth Manor and his brothers before leaving for the Palace.

He couldn't stand to face Nell again and lose control of himself. The determination to do the right thing drives him to flee far away to a location where she will never be allowed to enter.

"Percival," The Prince remarked with phony excitement, "My friend, I hope you are here to stay until the ball preparations are completed; otherwise, I will have to summon you."

Percival caught up on the Prince's mood fast, but as a lifelong friend, he knew to ignore it. The Prince always came around when he handled whatever was bugging him.

"I told the princess I'd assist with the preparations, and I will. Don't worry, my friend," Percival remarked, striding towards the ballroom.

"Keep in mind, it is my neck that will hang if you fail," The prince said as they walked side by side.

"I am sure both of our necks are on the line," Percival replied, laughing.

"No, I am confident Princess will forgive you," The prince whispered it in a faint whisper that only Percival could hear.

"And why is that?" He asked, not understanding.

"Have not you heard the rumors? She fancies you," the prince said casually.

"Don't tell me you believe idle rumor now. Of all the people in the Kingdom, you should know better," Percival remarked, staring at his buddy intently.

It was not the issue to be addressed in front of everyone, or even at all. Unfortunately, he had to reassure his buddy of his commitment to him. Finally, he was a prince who had spent his whole life surrounded by deception, and one misstep on his part may jeopardize their alliance.

"I am needed in the throne room, the princess will be here soon please make sure everything is moving smoothly," The prince muttered this while walking away.

Why did everything seem as if it was slipping away from him?

13

Chapter Thirteen

Nell could not believe her luck. She was to remain in London and care for Lady Adelaide while Addie was introduced to London society with Percival, a subtle indication that the Whitworth had discovered the future Duchess of Whitworth.

She was depressed; Percival had departed for the Royal Palace, and she hadn't seen him before leaving for Donovan, but now Lady Donovan had instructed her to wait on Lady Adelaide at Whitworth Manor. She was angry with the Whitworths and Donovans because they constantly forget other people's positions and backgrounds.

She was now at Whitworth Manor, waiting in her quarters for the party to arrive. She hadn't seen Percival in three days and wasn't sure whether he was at the estate or still in the palace. She used to be busy assisting Mrs. Fitzgerald on his estate, but there was nothing for her to do at Whitworth Manor. The support here was plenty and superior at what they performed, with her assistance seeming to be intrusive in their duty.

Sitting idle, her thoughts raced in many directions, eventually settling on one person. His smile and laughter, as well as his loving and calm demeanor, haunted her at all times. No one had ever been so attentive to her, and now that she had tasted it, she wanted it forever.

She was thrilled and glad for the opportunity to meet the Daviess and their children, but her attitude toward him shifted dramatically. He was now more kind and understanding. She had become used to his presence that his absence was causing her to feel restless.

When she went to see Lady Addie, the guilt trickled from her heart drop by drop. She was the same cheerful woman who was still attempting to befriend her, and she felt humiliated because she had prohibited emotions for the Lady's fiancé.

She wanted to avoid everything, even the mention of his name, so that the lunacy could end. The week passed with just murmurs about the pair in the hallway, with everyone waiting for Whitworth's engagement announcement. Every day, she would assist Lady Addie look her best for the Whitworths.

It should have helped her overcome her ridiculous infatuation, but her sentiments seem to have grown stronger with time. The parliament session was taking a two-week holiday for Christmas, and everyone was on their way back to Donovan's to celebrate together, hoping Lord Percival would ask Lady Adelaide to marry on Christmas Eve.

She was the last to depart after finishing up all of her remaining responsibilities in London; she would ride back to the estate in Donovan's carriage, never to return to London again. She will take a day off from anything that reminds her of Percival. She was looking forward to a fresh mind and a day of quiet.

She closed her eyes and laid back, resting while waiting for the driver to begin their trip. The door of her carriage opened, and she saw Percival standing in front of her. He observed her and his countenance changed to one of astonishment, which was also reflected on her face.

Nell soaked in the sight of him, her heart racing and a weight in her stomach rising up. He seemed ruggedly attractive in the light that reflected through the window. His black eyes darkened, urging her to get lost in his gloom.

"Nell," he said breathlessly.

She was tongue-tied, and her name rolled off his tongue like smooth velvet.

"My Lord, should we be on our way?" The driver said, breaking them out of the stupor.

Percival nodded, his gaze never leaving her.

"Milord," she murmured in a shaky voice.

He sat up straight in his seat, the astonishment on his face gone and the icy mask in its place. Nell knew something was amiss in her gut. He was the same, yet unique in certain ways.

"I apologize for intruding, Miss Nell," he remarked coldly. "I was caught up in the palace and didn't want others to wait for me. I didn't realize you were going back in Donovan's carriage; I'll arrange for another vehicle for myself. Good day."

He pounded on the carriage, signaling it to halt. Nell sat still, still recovering from the rush of emotion that had struck her. After a fortnight, she began to suspect he was not genuine; it was helping her ignore her emotions for him, and now that he was so close, her made-up walls were cracking.

He walked out of the carriage, leaving her astonished. She stayed still for a long time until she heard people outside. She couldn't understand what they were saying, but one distinct voice among them was growing closer, and her heart began to race.

Percival sat back in the carriage, rigid as a board, his mouth tightened as if he were trying to restrain himself. He knocked hesitantly, indicating the truck to go.

"I am afraid we will have to bear each other's company till we reach Donovan's estate," he replied.

The tension between them was evident. His position implied he was unhappy, and she didn't want to irritate him anymore. The uneasy quiet was becoming harder to endure. She never imagined he would be able to sit calmly for so long. Anything was preferable to this stillness; she missed fighting with him openly, and even his remorse sounded better than sitting under his gaze.

"I thought everyone was supposed to leave in the morning itself, milord," she broke the hush.

His piercing gaze fixed on her; his typical black eyes filled with rage.

"If you are accusing me of purposely sabotaging your ride then you are mistaken," he remarked with a smile.

"I am not accusing you of anything," She claimed her fury was rising, "It is simply unusual that you are not traveling with your family."

"Why do you even care?" He responded in a manner that matched her fury.

"Because I was supposed to be traveling alone with peace and quiet," she cried furiously.

"I wasn't the one who started this altercation," He said that he was equally upset. "I was sitting quietly, minding my own business. I did nothing to provoke you this time."

"Your mere presence is provoking," she blurted out without thinking.

A flicker of pain flashed over his face. The rage on his face was quickly replaced by a stoic expression, but his eyes still revealed the anguish he felt from her remarks. She sat back, wondering whether the stillness was any better before.

"I apologize; I had no idea my presence was so revolting to you," he muttered, his jaw clinched and turning away.

It crushed her heart to hear him say that while the truth was quite contrary. She had never needed anybody else's presence as much as she did his, and she knew she would never find someone like him again.

They sat in agonizing stillness, the need to leap out of the carriage strong in both of them. They were cramped in the little vehicle, their emotions pulling them closer together while their minds tried to keep them apart.

As evening descended, they would arrive at Donovan's by nightfall. Percival directed that the carriage be halted at the next tavern for leisure. He stepped forward, and the servants lined up to serve him. He requested tea to gain strength for the trek ahead. His rage had subsided, but the pain of being despised by her was causing him much more distress.

He didn't stay any longer than required; instead, he requested his carriage to be brought forward so that he may continue on his voyage. The sun was sinking, and the orange tint painted on the sky above illuminated everything on Earth, creating a stunning scene. And then he saw her, lighted by the sun's last rays, and lost his heart.

14

Chapter Fourteen

"Why do you hate me?"

She heard Percival speak clearly, but she didn't understand the significance of his query. His temperament has changed since their tavern visit. He remained gazing at her, setting all of her nerves on fire, but she couldn't sense any wrath coming from him anymore. And suddenly he asked her such a stupid question out of nowhere.

"Hate!" She laughed at the silliness of his question: "How can anybody ever dislike you, milord? You are the nicest and most lovely nobility I've met thus far. I've never heard anybody talk poorly of you; everyone admires and respects you. You meet the expectations of the heir to Whitworth. People in your company admire you, milord."

"Yes, or no?" He asked once more.

Her grin vanished. She talked favorably of him, but he was still stuck on his query.

"Milord, I told you ..." She said.

"No, you told me what others thought of me. I don't want to know what everyone thinks of me; I want to know whether you dislike me or not." He said angrily.

"Don't I come under everyone, milord?" She inquired, unsure of what he was thinking.

"No," he said simply.

Nell's heart sank in her gut. So, he regarded her like everyone else did: an abomination, the fruit of adultery, a prostitute's daughter. She assumed he considered her as nothing more than an average lady, but this was not the case, and her heart broke.

"Nell," He continued, breaking out of her daydream, "you did not answer my question."

"No, my Lord. I don't hate you," she answered, unable to keep the harshness out of her tone.

"I do not believe you," he murmured, his arms crossed and his gaze fixed on her.

"Does it matter?" She continued quietly, "Once we reach Donovan, you will never see my face again."

"See, this is why I don't believe you," He remarked, annoyed.

She said nothing. Time went slowly as she stared at her feet, and he continued to attempt to figure her out. She was like the most complicated puzzle that had ever existed.

"If you don't hate me then why are you always annoyed at me?" He asked.

"Because you annoy me," she said, glancing up.

Percival's mouth fell at her forthright response, and he broke out laughing after he had composed himself. His laughter tugged at her heartstrings. With the little time she had with him, she knew he seldom laughed so freely. He was usually smiling and pleasant, but his chuckle showed his genuine personality. She felt like she was losing herself even more.

"No one has ever complained that I annoy them, except you," he replied, still chuckling quietly. "Everyone has always liked my company."

"As you pointed out, milord, I do not come under everyone," she answered, puffing. Her eyes were once again fixed on her feet, attempting to quell the growing loathing she felt for herself.

"No, you don’t. You are special," he whispered quietly, looking at her.

"Like an abomination," she replied, oblivious to the expression in his eyes.

Percival was too astonished to speak another word. His thinking was a tangled mess. He attempted to talk, but couldn't think of anything to say. He leaned against his seat and attempted to get a handle on himself, realizing that saying anything now would only make things worse.

Nell despised the stillness between them, but every time she thought it was the worst, she was proven incorrect. This saddened her so profoundly that she didn't realize a tear had fallen from her eyes to her cheeks and her clasped hand. Tears streamed down her hands before she realized it, but the pain kept her still.

Her cheeks felt wrapped in warm hands, and her eyelids closed reflexively. Her head tilted up, and her thumb wiped the tears away from her cheeks. The fragrance of the forest after the rain, combined with something more, assaulted her nostrils, causing her to swallow.

"Nell," she recognized the lovely voice.

"Open your eyes," he instructed.

She clenched her eyes firmly, refusing to look into the obsidian eyes that made her forget everything. The darkness does not frighten her, but rather invites her to sink in it without concern.

"Nell," he murmured, his breath caressing her cheek. Her eyes opened without her consent, revealing her blue pools and his obsidian ones. His eyes, like usual, drew her full attention, and her heart began to race as his gaze left hers and went over her lips.

They were automatically drawn to onc other, his head bending slightly and their gaze fluttering near to a single goal.

Their lips lingered over one another, and their breath was ragged. Their lips almost touched against one another, sparking the burning heat that surged throughout their whole body.

The carriage jolted, and Nell fell on Percival's feet as he sought to save her.

"Nell," Percival said worriedly. "Are you okay?"

He helped her sit back and checked for any injuries.

"Are you hurt anywhere?" He asked, fusing over her.

"I am fine," she said gently, her eyes still downcast.

"Nell, look at me," He murmured, bringing her chin up.

"Are you hurt anywhere?" He asked sincerely.

"No," she answered, her pulse racing as he stared down at her. He smiled angelically, tucking a stray curl behind her hair.

"Stop," she shouted, yanking away from him.

"What's wrong?" He inquired worriedly.

"You need to stop, milord, whatever you are doing," she pleaded in despair.

"Alright, I will stop, please calm down," he murmured, attempting to soothe her. "I apologize if I made you uncomfortable."

Nell struggled hard with herself to regain control of her senses; the reality of what might have occurred threw her nerves into overdrive. Her emotions were in turmoil; she had never felt such intensity of emotions before.

Her eyes were filled with nightmarish flashbacks, and the revulsion of her mother's disgrace steadily swallowed her. She almost kissed him, making the same error of being involved with the aristocracy that had slain her mother.

Her horror seized her so completely that she forgot about her surroundings. When she eventually awoke from the terrifying abyss she had fallen into, she felt the warmth around her and the sweet murmurs of her name.

She flung him away as soon as she realized she was in Lord Percival's clutches, wrapping her arms around herself to protect herself from him.

"I apologize I was only trying to help you," He apologized and added, "Please, have some water."

She nervously took the water he provided. He sat staring out the window on the opposite side, leaving her to her own devices. After she calmed down, she felt humiliated for losing her senses in such a manner.

She reddened as she realized they were nearly kissing one other, which would have been dreadful given that he was already spoken for. She pondered how it might feel to be kissed by him and then chastised herself for thinking that way.

But her thoughts kept drifting to his obsidian eyes, which pierced her. Their lips are nearly touching. The kiss would have been a once-in-a-lifetime experience, and she wasn't sure whether she could have handled it. She was already infatuated with him, and the way he looked at her didn't help her resist her feelings. She needed to stop herself before she started down the road to her demise.

She couldn't help but think that even if they had kissed, it wouldn't have meant anything to him. After all, he was from Whitworth, and she was the daughter of a prostitute.

15

Chapter Fifteen

"Oh my, oh my, these kids are going to drown our reputation in controversies. Mr. Roberts? Where is Mr. Roberts?" Lady Donovan shouted to the maids performing the last sweep of the adorned ballroom, "Someone, go collect Mr. Roberts right now."

Mr. Roberts briefly introduced himself to the lady of the home.

"My ladies," he replied, bowing. "You asked for me."

"Mr. Roberts, look at all these hazardous plants hanging from every door and corner; kindly remove them wherever you find them. I don't want a single mistletoe in this house," said Lady Donovan, scanning around for another of the toxic plant that may have evaded her.

"Where did these dratted kiddies get the mistletoe, anyway? Mr. Roberts, please keep an eye on our children who refuse to grow up to their age," Lady Whitworth replied, angry.

"Where are our husbands, anyway? Have they neglected to keep an eye on their naughty youngsters while we take one final look at the preparation?" Lady Donovan asked.

Two women cursed their fully grown children and spouses, as Mr. Roberts calmly waited for the next order.

"Mr. Roberts, is everything ready?" Lady Donovan inquired worriedly.

"My ladies, everything is ready, I am personally keeping track of everything, so don't worry," Mr. Roberts remarked firmly.

"Even with these dratted children increasing the work," Lady Whitworth replied, seeing another mistletoe.

"I am sure, the Lordships will soon find other ways to entertain themselves, my ladies, rest assured," he remarked.

"Where is everyone?" Lady Whitworth inquired.

"His Lordships went for a gallop, my ladies, Lord Cedric is in the study and Lord Percival hasn't left his chamber," Mr. Roberts told the crowd.

"And Addie?" Lady Donovan asked.

"She is looking after the food preparations, my lady."

The Donovan estate mansion was bustling with excitement as everyone anticipated Christmas Eve. The Donovan mansion was magnificently decked like a fairy tale castle, and the folks within were looking forward to celebrating much more than Christmas Eve.

After many years, these two families were enjoying Christmas together without interference from neighboring households. Everyone was enjoying their time away from the scrutiny of society; they were regular people on vacation with their families, not the nobles who were watched by everyone.

Percival tried his hardest to enjoy himself since coming to Donovan's estate; when he couldn't, he pretended to be enthusiastic, but he couldn't do it any longer. He didn't want to damper others' spirits because of the storm developing in his soul. Everyone looked up to him with the anticipation of being engaged on Christmas Eve, and he was terrified someone would see the hesitancy in his eyes.

His mother's ring, a family treasure that had always graced the Lady of Whitworth's hand, felt heavy in his pocket. This ring would permanently cement his destiny with Adelaide, and he could feel his finger burning as he touched it. The Duke and Duchess of Whitworth were to serve the royal family, England's most significant aristocratic house, together.

His heart opposed the notion of Addie having the ring; he might follow in the footsteps of Edward, the 4th Duke of Whitworth, who never handed the ring to his wife since he was never in love with her, but would he be bold enough to do so?

His heart and head were at conflict with one another. His intellect was berating him to get over his obsession with Nell, propose Addie, and be prepared to accept his fate as the heir to Whitworth. He has to mend his friendship with the prince and join the King's council as his confidant. While his heart asked him to be selfish for a while and seek the one person who made him feel excited and happy.

The day started slowly than usual, with each passing instant adding to the apprehension. His valet began preparing him for the night. He wanted to pretend to be unwell and hide inside his room, hoping that Nell would come to take care of him as she had the previous time and he would be able to see her again. It's been a week since they landed at Donovan's, and he hasn't seen her since, the yearning driving him mad.

He spent the most of his time with his younger brothers rather than Addie, as everyone anticipated of him. Cedric saw his distance from Addie and questioned him, but he brushed it off since he would be spending the rest of his life with her and wanted to spend holidays with the whole family. Cedric was skeptical but did not trouble him after that.

Even though no one was coming to Donovan and Whitworth's for Christmas, the ballroom was adorned for dancing, with a feast set up at one end and an orchestra filling the space with wonderful tunes. Percival was the last to arrive, and he saw his parents dancing in the middle as everyone cheered them on. The military personnel were a welcoming audience who also enjoyed the festivities.

Before he could seek for Nell, Tavi pulled him into the dance floor, where he found Addie in his arms; she looked stunning, capturing the attention of everyone on the floor, but he felt nothing. He missed Nell's blue, cold eyes and wished she were the one he was hugging.

He complimented his parents for enjoying Christmas without others since there were five Lords and only one woman to dance with, and Addie was quickly out of his arms and into Felix'. His mother danced with Cedric. He positioned himself on the outside, away from the festivities but near enough that everyone noticed he was someplace else.

His melancholy attitude was brightened as Dom, Tavi, and Felix began singing Christmas carols as part of their surprise, and they quickly swept several of the attractive ladies onto the dance floor, making them flush from head to toe. But now he had to dance with Addie repeatedly, as well as with his mother and Aunt Genevieve, in order to avoid being near Addie. Every time she appeared in front of him, he felt like he was destroying both her and his own heart. The voices in his brain were now warring furiously.

Everyone was exhausted from all the dancing and caroling, so they ate a beautiful meal and sat around the fire, enjoying each other's company. Nobody appeared to notice that the Whitworth ring was still not on

Addie's finger. He purposefully left it in his bedroom, unable to take its weight.

"Percival," he said, looking up at Cedric who addressed him.

"Yes," he answered, emerging from the fantasy he had lost himself in.

"What is wrong?" Cedric inquired.

"Nothing," he said, noting the elder's withdrawal from the room.

"They retired for the night," Cedric replied to his unasked inquiry. "Do you have the ring with you?"

Percival tensed at his brother's inquiry.

"I'll make sure Felix, Tavi, and Dom excuse themselves until you return with the ring," Cedric murmured, his gaze fixed on him.

He groaned and went up the stairs to get the ring. He wished for a miracle the whole time so he wouldn't have to place the ring onto Addie's finger. He paused at the door, listening to the conversations within the ballroom and teasing the edge of the ring in his pocket.

As promised, Cedric ensured his brothers were gone since the only sound he heard was the rustling of a skirt from one end to the other. He shut his head and crushed his heart, repeatedly shouting that this was the correct thing to do. It was his responsibility, and duty comes before anything else.

With steely resolution, he entered the dimly illuminated ballroom, but his resolve disintegrated as he saw his heart's desire standing in front of him.

16

Chapter Sixteen

He was glued at the spot, soaking in the sight of her, her every movement making his pulse race in his chest. When their eyes met, his breath caught in his throat, and he felt his soul leave his body and float in the air, attempting to reach her. His legs moved on their own, his face adorned with the brightest grin and watery eyes, all of his emotions shown on his attractive face.

Nell stood there staring at him as if there was nothing else in the world except them. Their breath mixed, their eyes locked on one other, and before anybody knew it, his lips were on hers, and the fire they had just extinguished engulfed them in one sweep. His lips stroked over hers, gently cradling her face in his palms, while her hands grasped his arms, attempting to melt into him entirely.

They poured their hearts out into the kiss, attempting to express all they felt with just one kiss. The yearning and adoration flowed out of them in waves. They experienced a lifetime in a single kiss and didn't want to let go, but their lungs complained due to a shortage of oxygen.

They stood for a long time, their foreheads touching, their breath breathless. The clock struck midnight, marking the conclusion of Christmas Eve and the beginning of Christmas Day.

"Merry Christmas," he muttered.

"Merry Christmas," she murmured, laughing.

Her blue eyes met his obsidian orbs, which twinkled with water and reminded her of a starry night sky. She loved it and moved impulsively to kiss him again. It was slow and exploratory, with her arms tightening around his neck and his pulling her closer around the waist.

They remained standing in the center of the ballroom, none of them wanting to wake up from their lovely dream.

"Did you not come to the celebration?" He inquired, grateful that she was still in his arms and hadn't tossed him away.

"No, milord," she said quietly.

Perhaps the midnight magic kept them in love with one other.

"Percival, call me Percival," he begged.

She remained quiet for a long time, and he was terrified she'd draw away and reject him again.

"Percival," she gasped, her whole body quivering, as he wrapped her in a closer grip.

Her head lay on his chest, listening to his thundering heartbeats, while his hands caressed her back, sending shivers through her. His eyes closed automatically as he inhaled deeply.

"Dance with me," he whispered, keeping his eyes closed.

"I don't know how to," she replied, her voice muffled against his chest.

He untangled himself from her and walked back, while she looked gorgeous with a surprised expression on her face.

"Let me teach you then," He murmured, bowing in front of her.

She followed his example and curtsied. They walked closer together, never taking their gaze away from one other. Their hands were only inches apart yet never touched. They completed a full circle before bowing again. Percival grabbed her hand in his own, bringing her other hand to his shoulder as he gently grasped her waist.

He responded, "Match my steps," and she concentrated on his feet, attempting to emulate him.

"You should look in my eyes," He said softly.

"How will I match the steps if I look up?" She asked innocently, her gaze still locked on his feet.

"YOU WILL. Trust me," he said boldly.

She stared up into his eyes.

"I might step on your foot," she pouted.

"My foot can handle it," He chuckled.

"But it will be easier if I mimic your steps," she remarked, pouting.

"I want you to enjoy it," he whispered, drawing her closer.

"But.." she argued.

"If you speak another word, I will kiss you," he replied firmly. "Again." He continued after a moment.

Her face erupted in flush, from the point of her ears to her bright cheeks to her collarbone, and he resisted the impulse to nip and imprint her neck with affection.

They danced to the song of air and the quiet of the night, their hearts thumping like drums, bringing a fairy tale to life. They danced until their feet couldn't move any more, and they danced until they were satisfied.

"It is late," Nell murmured as the last flame flickered and they were enveloped in full darkness.

Percival took her hand and pulled her towards him, indicating her to follow him. She took a time to think before taking a step toward him. They immediately made their way through the black halls and stopped in front of his door. She paused, her hand sliding away from his. Her expression was one of anxiety.

"Nell," he said, "Trust me."

The enchantment began to shatter, and the charm was removed, but his honesty drew her in, and she entered his bedroom.

He set her down in the chair in front of the fire and tossed his waistcoat upon his bed. She looked about, trying to calm herself, fighting back the dread that threatened to engulf her whole. She reminded herself that he is a gentleman, and she trusts him. She trusts him. But, should she? The recollection of the carriage journey attempted to dispel any residual magic.

He sat down on the floor in front of her, gazing up at her with adoration in his eyes, forcing her demons to withdraw into the corner.

"Nell," he muttered.

"Yes," she said, gulping.

"I want you to do something for me tonight," he added, hoping.

Her cheeks became pale at his words. He softly gripped her hands, imploring her to trust him.

She nodded faintly.

"Close your eyes," he instructed.

She gazed at him with wide eyes. He gripped her palm again and nodded gently, encouraging her to shut her eyes. She gasped, hoping she would not have to repent trusting him.

She felt him move away from her, and then he grabbed her left hand and kissed the back of her palm. She felt something chilly slide through her finger, yet his warm palm still held hers.

"You can look now," he murmured.

She opened her eyes to find him staring at her hand, a large green stone glinting on her finger. She was startled beyond words. It was very incorrect. She was dumbfounded.

"I wanted to see how it looked in its proper place," she overheard him remark quietly.

"I can't, and it shouldn't," she attempted to say.

"I know," He continued, glancing at her, "Only for tonight, just for tonight."

He looked at the stone glinting on her finger for a long time before finally falling asleep on her lap as she gently ran her fingers over his hair.

She would never forget this night. She felt at peace, protected, and loved, and she was willing to give her soul to the devil for a night like this with him till she died.

She went down and gave him a delicate kiss on the head, his steady breathing stroking her hand, which he securely held before falling asleep. She sat there staring over him, etching the memory in her mind till morning. The fairytale was coming to an end.

He was sleeping deeply, so it pained her to wake him up before anybody discovered her in his room. He was partly asleep as she moved him to bed with some difficulty, tucking him in and kissing his forehead one more time.

Percival awoke, shocked. He found himself on his bed, even though he was certain he had not fallen asleep there. She was gone, her scent still clinging on his garments, and the green diamond gleamed on the side table.

17

Chapter Seventeen

Nell quietly closed the door on her way out, finally releasing the breath she'd been holding all night. She rested her head against the door, all the strain in her body dissolving. She had to empty the ballroom before anybody awoke, like she was supposed to do last night.

She felt butterflies in her stomach as she remembered last night's kiss and dance; everything was a dream, and she couldn't believe she was fortunate enough to live in a fairy tale, no matter how incorrect it was or how soon her demons would consume her. However, the memory will always be pristine, and she will continue to enjoy these exquisite sensations for as long as she can before succumbing to the darkness of her actions.

But destiny dealt her a harsh hand when she met the fiancée of the guy she had abandoned.

"Follow me," she overheard Addie say. She watched her go away, and Nell felt like she was headed to the gates of hell, and she could deserve what was coming to her.

She trailed after Addie, her thoughts colliding together. She stood inside her room for a long time, staring at Addie's back as she looked out the window, the first rays of day finally appearing.

Both ladies stood in complete quiet, with Nell flinching at each slightest sound that reached her ears. The chirping of the birds and crowing of the crows, the rustling of the leaves in the early wind, her protected haven was transforming into her own manufactured hell. She was staring at her feet, her fists firmly clutched together, and she was trying not to close her eyes and cover her ears with her hands, screaming her heart out.

"Look at me," she heard Addie whisper quietly, and she felt like crying. She was overwhelmed with guilt and revulsion.

"Nell, look at me," Addie urged, her patience fading.

She glanced up, anticipating fury and scorn, but her heart wrenched when she saw Addie's pained face and didn't know how to respond. She understood how to deal with disdain and wrath, but pain made her vulnerable, and the gravity of what she had done struck her full force. She should never have followed her heart; it led her to hurt someone else.

"Aren't you going to say anything?" Addie muttered as her tears were about to pour.

Nell opened her lips to say something, anything, but she couldn't find any words to describe the tempest within her.

"Despite what everyone thought, I always believed you are nothing like your mother," Addie continued with a smile. "Don't make me regret believing in you."

Nell's eyes welled up with tears; she wanted to apologize, but it felt little in comparison to the pain she had caused Addie.

"Remember one thing Nell, you could never become anything more than a mistress or maybe that's what you want to be," Addie spoke out again after a moment: "Now get out."

Nell stood paralyzed, unable to move a single muscle. Addie groaned and exited her room.

Nell needed to get away from here. When she regained consciousness, she found herself on the floor, her weeping unrestrained, and the first snow falling outside. She bolted from Addie's room like she was on fire, despite the cold that had permeated into the chamber and her bones.

She struggled her way through the pouring snow, having been trekking for hours and being completely unconscious of her surroundings. Her feet were burned, and her torso had frozen. She found herself in front of an orphanage. She felt relieved since her brain was screaming for the agony in her body rather than the anguish in her heart.

When she opened her eyes again, she was in a dirty room with a strong disinfectant odor that made her gag. She was in anguish, with every nerve in her body on fire. She attempted to sit up to identify the room she had woken up in, but the bowl near her clattered to the floor with a loud sound.

"Ah, you are awake," someone whispered from her right. "Sit still now. Let me bring the mixture."

A small child held a combination in front of her nose, and she cringed at the fragrance.

"You have a fever, missy, drink it, and you will feel better," He stated, pushing the unpleasant mixture at her.

"Where am I?" She asked, her voice husky.

"D. Bennett's clinic, missy," He said, "You were chilled almost to death. How did you wind up in that abandoned building? You should be cautious; the folks strolling about are not to be crossed with. You were fortunate I was looking for herbs for the doctor and came upon you."

"Thank you," she responded, "I would like to go back."

"Eleanor," He murmured, annoyed and ready to refuse her, but her look told him she wouldn't listen. "Alrighty, I will take you back to your home."

She was thankful to the sweet lad who handed her his pony as he went in front of her, talking away as she steered him to the mansion. She quickly realized everything was quiet, and she opened her weary eyes to find the Donovan mansion in front of her. The child stared at the gigantic building, his mouth gaping.

"What is your name?" She asked faintly.

"Huh," he muttered, without glancing away from the mansion. "Hec."

He coughed and stared at her back.

"Hector," he murmured with surprise in his eyes. "You live here. This is like the King's palace."

"Are you new in the county?" She asked again.

"Yes," he responded. "My father died a week ago, and I had nowhere else to go except to my cousin, Dr. Bennett's wife. I arrived last week."

Nell led him down the back road to the stable as the sun was lowering on the horizon. The stable master told Nell that he would feed Hec and set up his bed for the night.

She staggered down the halls and made it to her room to sleep off her fever and tiredness, but she was soon visited by the Lady of the manor, who was accompanied by her butler, Mr. Roberts. She was filled with fear, ready to be cast out of the manor, and the embarrassment that would come with dallying with the Whitworth heir made her head spin.

"Where were you?" Lady Genevieve said, "And what happened to you? Why are you looking so pale?"

"I became ill, milady," Nell answered faintly. "I didn't want to bother anybody, so I was on my way to see Dr. Bennett for medication, but my condition deteriorated. I returned as soon as I was myself; Dr. Bennett's assistance, Hec is in the stable; he brought me here, milady."

The falsehoods came out of her tongue, leaving a foul taste, and she pleaded for forgiveness for her dishonesty.

"You had us worried," Lady Genevieve replied, lowering her voice. "Do not disappear on your own like that ever again, Nell."

Lady Genevieve cautioned that she could already sense a break in the trust she had built since starting work at Donovan's manor. She could hear everyone stating that her parents' sins didn't matter, yet here they were eager to criticize her and put her in the same category as her mother at the slightest indication of a mistake.

She felt much better after the night's sleep and returned to work the following day, but everyone's eyes were filled with mistrust and suspicion like never before. They used to assume she was like her mother, but now they were beginning to believe it.

Lady Addie seemed to have talked with no one, which added to her embarrassment. Everyone was watching her like a hawk, but no one had questioned her yet. Mr. Roberts informed her that she would be working in the kitchen rather than attending to Lady Addie.

She was no longer the Lady's friend, but rather a servant, and it was probably best if she avoided everyone.

18

Chapter Eighteen

Percival spent the whole Christmas morning feigning and acting excited to exchange presents. He found it difficult to maintain the illusion throughout the day, but he quickly learned he wasn't the only one pretending. He discovered Aunt Genevieve and Addie in anguish, which was undoubtedly his fault, and he couldn't help but feel terrible. Everyone expected him to announce his engagement, but he was still hesitant.

He sensed Cedric's uncertainty and displeasure. He spent all of his time with his father discussing their new probable enterprise, shunning everyone else. His parents were unexpectedly unconcerned with his delaying his engagement, and he couldn't be more thankful for this favor.

His brother nabbed him while they were on their way to supper.

"What is going on, Percival?" Cedric murmured.

"Nothing is going on," Percival murmured, attempting to get away.

"Why haven't you proposed?" Cedric inquired once again. "Yesterday night was the perfect opportunity."

Percival did not respond to his query, but his brother's next comment made him angry.

"I hope you remember what is expected of you, Percival," Cedric went on to say.

Percival's steps came to a standstill as wrath poured out of him.

"You mean what is expected of a Whitworth heir," He responded, his voice rising, "I am well aware of it; you don't need to remind me."

"Calm down," Cedric murmured, lifting his hand to signify that he didn't intend to irritate him.

"Maybe you should talk it out in private; we will buy you time at the table," Dom murmured behind them, beside Tavi.

"There is no need for it, Dom," Percival remarked, walking away to the dining room.

Everyone around the table, with the exception of Percival, was animated. Dom and Tavi ensured that no one addressed Percival directly, keeping the table engaged.

"We should all go to the picnic near the waterfall; the water should be frozen. We can all skate," Felix said. Everyone warmly supported Felix's plan.

"What about you, Percival?" Lady Seraphina questioned her firstborn.

"I was thinking about returning to London. I have to assist the Royal Highnesses with the ball preparation," Percival began, making everyone's face fall, "If it is possible, I would like to ask Addie to join me for the New Year's ball at Duchess Everly."

Everyone let out a breath of relief, and their faces lit up like Christmas. The Duchess Everly Ball was the pride of London, the finest ball after the Queen's, and it was an excellent way to introduce the future Duchess of Whitworth to London society.

"I think it's best all of us stay here, let both of them take a breath without anyone of us hovering over," she remarked. Everyone agreed to Lady Seraphina's proposition, and Percival felt a big load lifted off his shoulders.

Everyone returned to their chambers in a cheerful mood. After saying their goodbyes to everyone, they set off for London the following day. Percival pretended to be sleeping during the ride, and Addie did not disturb him once. He was dismayed when her Lady maid was someone other than Nell, but he figured it was for the best.

It was best for him, as the Whitworth heir, to keep as far away as possible from her. He couldn't stay with her forever, therefore he needed to perform his job by presenting an ideal woman to society as the Duchess of Whitworth. He determined to accompany Addie to the Duchess Everly ball as his betrothed, and nothing less.

He purchased another ring to propose to Addie since he couldn't gift his mother's ring to the lady who would never be his. He had the ring in his pocket, trying to muster the strength to seal his destiny, but Nell's face kept flashing before him, and he couldn't bring himself to give up. He intended to do it during Duchess Everly's ball, but he failed once again, leaving Addie at her wits end.

They returned to the mansion, and he walked away to his room without saying anything to her.

"My Lord," she murmured, causing him to stop in his tracks.

"I can't play your games anymore, my Lord," Addie remarked, her expression filled with agony, "I can't keep waiting for you to propose marriage. It is horrible for a girl to beg for a proposal, and I can't pretend that everything will be good when I believe you are hesitant about this relationship. You have the freedom to do anything you want, but I'm running out of time and can't keep waiting for something that will never come my way."

"I am sorry," he murmured, torn between remorse for Addie and love for Nell.

"You made me feel so desperate and unworthy, my Lord," Addie murmured in a weak voice, leaving him standing in the entryway.

Addie was up and packing before dawn, after looking at the ceiling all night. She was leaving Whitworth Manor empty-handed once again, and she had no idea how she would deal with Donovan's return home. She failed as a daughter to her parents and guardians, again.

Percival was waiting in the foyer, bags under his eyes, his hair tangled, and exhaustion radiating from his face. He didn't sleep all night, and when his valet told him that Addie had requested that the carriage be readied for Donovan at the crack of dawn, he needed to make a choice quickly. He stood in front of the Lady he had let down, unsure if he actually wanted to spend his life with her.

He constantly witnessed how much his parents loved and respected one other. He would be demeaning his marriage and his wife if he couldn't give her his best as a husband. He had a responsibility as Whitworth heir to choose a deserving lady to be Duchess of Whitworth, but he couldn't fulfill his obligation to Addie or any other woman as a husband since he was in love with Nell.

But he also knew he could never be with Nell; he couldn't risk jeopardizing the Whitworth name by realizing his heart's longing. Nell could be the purest thing in the world, but her name and blood would bring the Whitworth name to disgrace, and he could never let that happen as long as the Whitworth reputation was on his shoulders.

His mind was inundated with all of these ideas at once, and the brandy he drank at night didn't help much. When he watched Addie go, he realized he had one final opportunity to make things right with her. The last opportunity to choose to follow the road that had been created for him.

"Addie," he began. "I need you to listen to me."

"You are drunk," she said startled, smelling the whiskey on his breath.

"I apologize, I apologize for everything but I need you to give me one last chance," he said.

"I will listen to you, my Lord," she responded with a hardened heart.

"We do not fancy each other, that much is very clear and it is my duty to choose a perfect lady to be the Duchess of Whitworth and I can't think of anyone else but you to fulfill that position," He swallowed and offered the ring to her. "Will you marry me?"

She gazed at him with disbelief and sorrow.

"You are offering me marriage as heir to Whitworth yet the ring is not the one Duchess of Whitworth wear, neither can you accept me as your wife," she replied with a tear in her eye.

"Addie," he implored.

"I refuse, my Lord," she responded. "I cannot be so desperate that I am ashamed of myself. Goodbye, my Lord. I hope you can choose between your heart and your responsibility and prevent many others from sorrow."

19

Chapter Nineteen

Nell quickly grasped why the duchess kept her apart from the housekeepers. It was her first time joining the house staff for dinner, and there was pin-drop stillness; it seemed like everyone was communicating to one other via their eyes, and no one dared to look at her or be near her as if she were a sickness.

One supper was enough for her to spend the remainder of the time in her own room; despite being demoted, she still had her room to herself; she was unsure how long she would have this luxury. The following few days were uncomfortable at best, but everyone was too busy preparing for the New Year, and with each new activity that enticed the visitors every day, no one had time to pay attention to Nell. She kept away from everyone and completed the chores given to her quickly.

She was always being observed, with one or both of them hoping to catch her making a mistake. She got the unsettling impression that her time at Donovan's estate was coming to an end. She would soon make a mistake, or be pushed to make one, and be tossed out into the streets. However, she never imagined herself being homeless in a couple of days.

It was the third day following the New Year, and she entered the kitchen to have her breakfast before taking over her chores from the housekeeper. Normally, the kitchen would be abandoned for a long time, and she would make sure she was the first in and out before anybody else, but today, the whole crew was there, talking amongst themselves. Some of them were partly sleeping, but their expressions were eager to hear what was undoubtedly going on above.

She was astonished that no one spotted her hanging near them, so she began to walk away when she heard someone scream out engagement and others shushing. Her heart was heavy as they spoke about the engagement. They must be anticipating the big news of Percival and Addie's marriage. Her trance was shattered by the foreboding clang of the bell, which summoned Mr. Roberts to the parlour.

Everyone remained quiet, waiting for Mr. Roberts to return and bring life back to everyone. Nell's anxiousness increased as she glanced around and saw everyone's downcast expressions. Something wasn't right. Everyone was supposed to be enthusiastic and cheery while waiting for the news, but that wasn't the case whatsoever.

Nell stood calmly in the back, tucking her quivering hands under her skirt and fighting to maintain her stern demeanor. When Mr. Roberts came downstairs and told the footmen to start packing all of the Whitworths' and be ready to depart for London by noon, none of them moved.

"Did you not hear me?" Mr. Roberts yelled again at the gaping footmen.

"Roberts, calm down, will ya?" Mrs. Hayes spoke. Mrs. Hayes was as old as the Donovan mansion; she was the daughter of the previous housekeeper and had spent her whole life at the manor serving the Donovans, running the home like a military commander with greying hair and wrinkled skin.

"So, what are you all waiting for? Go and start working on your chores," she said again.

"But, Mrs. Hayes," a handmaid complained. "What happened upstairs?"

"She came without the engagement ring, I saw her," a person said hurriedly. "Her eyes were red as a fire from crying."

"I was hoping she would get married this season," an older maid commented, "Poor lad, firstly an orphan and now on a shelf."

"Now, everyone go back to work right now," Mrs. Hayes said, "I don't want to hear another word of it. If I catch someone talking, they will thoroughly clean every room."

Everyone hurried to eat their breakfast and return to work. Nell stood there, slightly trembling.

"Roberts," Mrs. Hayes replied, "Don't forget that what occurs upstairs should not interfere with our responsibilities. Go take a minute and return to your post."

"Nell," Mrs. Hayes shouted out to Nell, who stood wide-eyed. "Go see Lady Addie. We don't have a new handmaid for her yet, and you look like the best alternative given your prior attendance. Stop standing there like a stupid idiot, and take her ladyship's breakfast."

Nell walked dumbfounded; the dish of food pressed into her hands. As she approached Lady Addie's door, which she had been avoiding since the previous time she was caught red-handed, she was about to speed past it when the Duchess saw her and beckoned her inside with breakfast.

"Nell," Lady Genevieve said, "Make sure she eats everything. I will be back shortly."

Nell waited in the corner, her head dipped low, while Addie gazed at her after Lady Genevieve had left them alone.

"Nell," Addie said quietly, "come here."

"Milady," she remarked with astonishment in her voice.

"Come sit near me," Addie requested.

Nell approached the four-poster bed and stood uncomfortably.

"Tell me, is it only Percival or are you infatuated with him too?" Addie inquired frankly.

"I'm sorry," Nell whispered, her voice faltering and tears flowing down her cheeks. She was shouting her apologies, feeling completely awful. She had no idea she was encompassed in Addie's arms, comforted by the lady whose future had been shattered as a result of her irresponsibility.

After Nell's sobbing stopped, Addie forced her onto her bed and sat at the other end, the breakfast tray laying between them.

"I always felt we were similar," Addie stated after a lengthy period of quiet.

"We couldn't be more different than two people in this world, milady," she said.

"We are both orphans," Addie remarked, rejecting Nell's comment. "And we both can't be with the man we love."

"You can, milady," Nell answered firmly. "I'm sure Lord Whitworth will see sense soon enough."

"Oh, no," Addie murmured with a sorrowful grin, gazing up at Nell. "I'm not in love with Percival, Nell, but I hope he doesn't come to his senses if it means denying his heart."

"You are not," Nell answered, astonished by the lady's reaction. "Then who?"

Nell inquired, unable to keep her interest to herself. Addie giggled at Nell's confused expression.

"Sorry, milady," she said hurriedly, "It is not my place to ask and I feel miserable that my careless actions hurt you."

"The only thing that hurts me is that Donovan's took me in, gave me a home and a family, treated me like a daughter, and never expected anything from me. They merely wanted me to marry a respectable guy and be the daughter they had always imagined I was," Addie remarked regretfully.

"You will still be their daughter with or without a man," Nell replied, not fully comprehending Addie.

"Not when they find out why my suitors didn't offer me marriage in my first two seasons," Addie remarked with a laugh.

Nell sat in quiet while Addie ate her breakfast. They had stopped talking to one other. When Addie asked Nell if she may ask her a personal question, Nell scooped up the tray and left.

"I will try to answer, milady," Nell answered hesitantly.

"You fancy him," Addie said hesitantly. "Uh, I don't know how to ask this?"

After a lengthy moment, Addie blurted out, her eyes closed.

"You spent the night with Percival, you fancy him and he fancies you, how does..." Addie was about to question her when an angry voice from the door stopped them.

"What!!" Felix bellowed.

"Felix," Addie said, scared.

Nell's cheeks paled as she saw the young master of the estate seem enraged at her, and she recalled what Addie had said. He must have just heard her final words, and she hated her destiny once again.

"You, whore," Felix snarled at Nell, "You are the reason for all this."

"Felix, no," Addie responded, approaching Felix. "You are misunderstanding."

"I heard you perfectly clear, Addie," Felix exclaimed furiously, heading out to tell others what he had heard.

"Felix, no, wait, listen to me," Addie dashed after Felix to stop him.

Nell stood with blood rushing to her ears and her head thumping violently.

There was just one thing on her mind: run.

20

Chapter Twenty

Nell found herself on the road, barefoot and wandering through newly fallen snow, with a tiny bag. Her mind was blank, save for the need to escape the place she never wanted to leave. Each stride separated her from all she knew and filled her with fear, but turning back was no longer an option. She knew what was behind her, and now she had to be bold and see what was ahead.

She just knew she was traveling to London. She was heading to the Daviess, the folks who had reared her and were the only family she had. She knew she could always turn to Mrs. Davies for consolation and then determine what her future held. She came to a standstill as she realized she was about to leave the country and never return.

She turned around to take one final glance at where she grew up. She never ventured outside the confines of the orphanage, but she always felt secure here. The dread of the unknown in the outside world has always kept her confined to this spot, and now she must go.

The Donovan mansion was visible far away, prompting her to turn around and go faster. She was so caught up in her inner anguish that she failed to see the rider who passed her. While she continued her stroll, she watched the rider in front of her come to a halt, turn around, and approach her. Her thoughts begged to flee again, but she stood firm despite every voice in her body screaming at her.

"Eleanor," the rider replied with a familiar tone.

"Hector," Nell replied, uncertain of his face concealed below the leather lapels that protected him from the cold.

He got off the horse, took off his hat, and smiled brightly. Nell calmed down when she saw a familiar face.

"Why is it that I always find you freezing, missy?" He asked.

Nell felt the bitter cold sink into her as she finally let her body release the strain she had been holding since leaving the estate. Her fingers were icy and she was shaking, so she giggled at him; he always finds her when she runs away.

"Now, where are you off to this time, missy?" He inquired when Nell did not respond.

"Where are you off to, Hec?" She requested in response.

"The big city, missy, London," he said excitedly at the idea of seeing London. He turned his horse around and began walking with Nell at his side.

"I was delighted when Dr. Bennett asked me to travel to London and purchase some drugs and deliver his letter to some of his medical pals. I inquired about to see what there was to look at; I didn't want to miss anything. I heard the Thames will be frozen at this time," Hec said, and Nell found consolation in it. He was a simple guy who wondered about everything. She momentarily questioned why she couldn't be as free as he was.

"Eleanor, you didn't tell me where you were going?" He asked again after a while.

"London," she said.

"On foot?" He inquired, amused. "The palace people didn't give you a pony." He was referring to Donovan Manor.

"I'm going to meet my guardians. No pony from the palace for personal use, Hector," she said.

"Well then, my ma always taught me to protect a woman in need and I am sure the road to London is not safe for a lone woman. I will come with you till you reach your guardian's home, missy," he answered firmly.

"Thank you for the offer but I will only slow you down," she added.

"You are in luck, missy, I have enough money to rent another horse so you won't slow me down, "He remarked.

Hector leased Nell another horse, and they were soon on their way to London. Hector performed the most of the talking, steering Nell away from her negative ideas. After half of the voyage, he got bored of conversing alone with no reaction from her, so they continued in quiet. They spent the night at a tavern stables a few miles outside London to escape the dangers of London's streets at night.

They resumed their journey at sunrise. Nell informed Hector that she was an orphan, and her guardians were the caretakers of the orphanage, which was the dilapidated structure where he last saw her. As they got closer, Hector informed her he lied and used his boarding money to hire a horse for her, which instead of infuriating her made her immensely thankful to him.

After berating him, Nell assured him that she would seek his boarding at the orphanage; their connection was similar to that of a younger brother and older sister. Hector was like a guardian angel to her, arriving whenever she got lost.

The orphanage was dreary, so Nell went inside and began seeking for Mrs. Davies, the one person who could hug her and allow her to scream her heart out. She was taken to Davies's quarters, which she entered by pounding on the door.

Mr. Davies was seated in the corner, looking worse than ever, with hollow cheeks and black eyes; he was a skeleton, his health worse than the last time she saw him. The grief in her heart intensified; he took her into his house when her own mother abandoned her, provided food and shelter, and stood up to everyone for her, and now she was back, bringing only troubles. She was about to turn around and go when Mr. Davies called her.

"Nell, is that you?" He inquired in a raspy voice that hadn't been used in a long time.

"Mr. Davies, yes," Nell said, "I.., Uh, where is Mrs. Davies?"

"What!" He inquired unfocusedly, the book in his hand slipping, his face pallid.

"Mr. Davies, are you alright?" She inquired, expressing worry.

"You don't know," he admitted defeat. Nell had no idea what he was talking about; he peered into oblivion, ignoring her existence, and she wanted to leave him to his own ways and hunt for Mrs. Davies.

"Uh, Mr. Davies, I will go look for Mrs. Davies," Nell responded hesitantly.

"She is gone," he said with a sigh. "She waited for you, she kept waiting, and when you didn't come, she left."

Nell was unsure what to make of Mr. Davies, but she was certain that Mrs. Davies would never abandon her husband.

"Mr. Davies, I'm sure she's here somewhere; I'll go look for her," Nell said.

"Nell," he groaned sadly, "Bring that box," he continued, pointing to the wooden box on the table.

Nell groaned and gently placed the package on his lap. Mr. Davies grabbed her wrist and asked her to sit near his feet. He remained mute, peering into space with one hand on her wrist and the other on the box. She became worried because Mr. Davies was behaving unusually.

"We had a baby after a decade of trying," he continued, startling Nell, "And then that happiness was taken away from us. It was quite challenging for us. People abandoned their children on our doorstep when we couldn't have our own. She was becoming worse by the day, and I felt like a failure. And then you arrived, and I removed you from the lady who gave you birth. You were so little and lovely, and when I placed that small bundle in her lap after the burial, she sobbed for the first time, and I knew you would bring her back to me." A shadow of a grin appeared on his face.

Nell's eyes streamed with tears. She knew what was coming, but she didn't want to believe it.

"She waited for you. I wrote multiple mails and received no response. We were scared, and I couldn't leave her alone to seek for you. She was delirious, sobbing for her baby. We had a boy, and she was weeping for a girl, and one night she left me all alone in this world," Mr. Davies recalled, tears streaming down his cheek.

Nell was weeping on Mr. Davies's lap as he held her hand. She had her head on his lap, looking at the burning candle, her soul numb with grief at the loss.

21

Chapter Twenty-one

Percival felt hollow. A piece of his heart had been gone, and he wasn't sure whether he wanted to feel whole again.

He couldn't remain at the Whitworth mansion or return to his land since Nell haunted every location he could think of. He considered going to the castle, but he wasn't sure whether his buddy was still upset with him, and the Princess still stared at him as if he hung stars for her.

How could he screw everything up in only a few months? He wrecked his own heart by falling in love with the lady he couldn't have, he ruined another's remaining future, and for the first time in 30 years, his closest buddy was disappointed and upset with him.

He had spent the night thinking and drinking, and now he felt completely ill, the voices in his brain so loud that he believed he was going mad. He had been nurtured his whole life to serve on the King's council alongside the Prince, and his position suddenly seemed to be shaky. The self-reproach was hurting him inside, and he didn't know which wound to treat first, so he drank till he passed out, allowing the brief serenity to flood his head.

He awoke with his head throbbing and felt worse than before. He was happy that the voices in his thoughts had gone quiet for a little period. His headache was so severe that he could not think clearly.

It was dark outside, and he seemed to be unaware of the time of day. He called for his valet and requested him to fetch something for his head.

"My Lord, his Lordship is asking for you downstairs," his valet remarked.

"His Lordship! Father is back?" Percival inquired, perplexed.

And, like a sledgehammer to his head, he recalled how Addie had left the Whitworth manor, and for the first time, he feared stepping up to his parents.

"Addie left this morning, how can they arrive so early?" He considered his head deterioration.

"My Lord," his valet said cautiously, "Lady Addie left yesterday morning, my Lord."

"No, that is not true, look out, the night is falling," he murmured, uncertain of himself.

"My Lord, you drank till the evening hours and you have been sleeping for more than 24hrs now," said his chauffeur.

Percival slumped down in the chair, his hands to his face, swallowing a yell of fury. His valet groaned; he'd been Lord Percival's valet for 12 years and had never seen him so dejected.

"My Lord, you are poorly; if I may, I shall tell his Lordship that you are ill. I've instructed the chef to make something for your head, and your bath will also be prepared. You should sleep after your supper, my Lord. You'll be fine by tomorrow morning," his valet offered.

Percival's jumbled brain concluded it was best to sleep off than confront his family's disappointed expressions.

After his valet finished fretting and giving him nasty medication for his head, he was about to return to his bed when his door burst open, revealing an enraged Cedric.

"Will," Percival heard Dom's voice somewhere down the halls and quickly arrived behind him, along with Tavi.

All three of them stood at the entrance, staring at him.

"What is it?" Percival inquired.

"Nothing; we came to see whether you needed a doctor or not. Your valet said you are ill," Dom remarked quickly before anybody else could.

"Really, Percival?" Cedric inquired aggressively.

"Will, no, you can talk tomorrow," Dom growled at his elder brother, while Tavi remained silent.

"Leave. Both of you," Cedric instructed Dom and Tavi.

"No. Look at him; he is not well." Dom argued, "You're coming with us."

"You must be exhausted from traveling; go rest. I'll talk to Cedric," Percival remarked to Dom and Tavi. While Dom was about to argue, Tavi tugged him away.

"Cedric, I am not sure why you are so furious with me. If not Addie, I can find another lady to marry," Percival murmured, rubbing his temples.

"Who? Nell!" Cedric replied, tauntingly freezing Percival in his position.

"How do you...." Percival was taken aback.

"How do I know?" Everybody knows. The whole Duchy of Donovan is aware, and by tomorrow's Gazette, the entire London will be aware, with Whitworth's name emblazoned beside the Hawthorne whore," Cedric said.

"She is not a whore," Percival said.

"Isn't she?" Cedric responded in a tone that matched his rage.

Both brothers were gazing daggers at each other.

"I dare you to say another word against her," Percival replied angrily.

"She seduced you like a whore, and like a fool, you let her," Cedric added, his voice low and disgusted.

And with that, Percival hit Cedric in the face, and Cedric responded by kicking him in the stomach; within a minute, both brothers were at each other's necks. When Dom and Tavi entered the room to separate them, the furniture was half-broken, and both men were hurt to varying degrees.

Everyone was quiet, with the Whitworth parent sitting near the fire and Cedric and Percival in two corners watched by Tavi and Dom, respectively.

"Montague, I can't," Lady Seraphina said, fatigued. "I am tired."

"What is going on, children?" Lord Montague inquired, the age appearing on his face for the first time and filling all his children with remorse, "Your mother and I did not raise you like this. You don't fight your brothers like a commoner; we trained you better."

"We are sorry, father," Dom added.

"Now that my children are adults, I trust their judgment to settle the matter internally. We are fatigued after the voyage, so we will depart first. Have a pleasant night," Lord Whitworth requested, holding Lady Seraphina's hand in his.

"Father, wait," Percival said, grabbing a package and presenting it to his parents.

"It is the Whitworth ring," she continued. "Percival, it is yours to give to the lady you will marry."

"It is more than that," Lord Montague said. "It is the pride of the Duchess of Whitworth and the woman who holds the heart of Duke of Whitworth."

"I can't give it to her," Percival replied, putting the package in his mother's hands.

"Nell," Lady Seraphina gasped.

"I am in love with her," he exclaimed out loud, his heart racing.

"You are spouting nonsense," Cedric said fiercely.

"And I know I can't have her," Percival said, a ghost of a grin on his lips. "Nobody has to worry; I know my responsibilities and will carry them out as expected of me."

Everyone was startled into stillness. No one knew what to say; Percival was in so much agony, yet he was gladly sacrificing his love with a grin.

"This is unfair," Dom said. "We are Whitworth; what is impossible for others, we can make possible for ourselves." Surely, there's a way."

"She is a prostitute's daughter, no one will accept it," remarked Octavian. "Apart from the blow to our reputation, Percival's place in the King's council and Cedric's place in the parliament will be in danger."

"Weren't you the one who scoffed at Donovan when they hesitated to provide her employment?" Dom questioned Tavi with a furrowed brow.

"It is one thing to provide employment to the woman in need and a completely different thing to keep her as a mistress," Tavi remarked in response to the accusation. "There are numerous women that will be more than willing to be a Whitworth mistress, Percival can choose from one of them."

Percival laughed, and everyone was quiet once again.

"I know she would rather die than be anyone's mistress, and I love her enough not to dishonor her by making her my mistress," Percival remarked after a little pause.

"You want to marry her," Lord Montague said, stunned.

Percival felt the emptiness overwhelm him as he saw the expressions in his family's eyes, as if he had lost his mind.

22

Chapter Twenty-two

Two days had gone since that night, and the mansion remained eerily still. His parents pushed them to have breakfast and supper together every day in the hopes that Percival and Cedric would ultimately confront one other and end their animosity. His parents initially pushed everyone together when they were kids, and Dom and Tavi avoided each other after a quarrel over a broken toy.

Percival felt it hilarious that his parents always made them handle their conflicts with each other rather than allowing them to build up. Maybe that was why his brothers were so close, constantly having one other's backs since there was no unresolved issue between them.

As far as he could remember, he had never fought Cedric, and he wanted to settle their issue, but he couldn't hear anything uttered against Nell. He was already suffering and swearing that he would never be able to be with her. His love would always be unrequited, and Cedric's behavior irritated him even more.

He was seated at one more forced breakfast, and Dom did his hardest to get everyone chatting, but without Tavi's humor, he failed terribly. Dom and Tavi had always been close, but they were now separated. The load on Percival's heart got heavier as he gazed around the table.

"I apologize," Percival said, "For putting you all through this."

"Percival, darling," Lady Seraphina responded, "You do not have to apologize for anything."

"No, mom. I need to apologize. I am really sorry for raising my hand on my brother; you raised us better than that. I am the oldest, and I should have known better. I apologize for inflicting such pain on both of you. I have disappointed you." Percival expressed regret.

"I apologize to you, Cedric, for being so thoughtless and careless. But I will not accept that you talked so negatively of the lady I am in love with. She did not choose to be born under such circumstances, and you have no right to condemn her for it. She did not seduce me; I was the one who sought her. I can't imagine all the pain she must be going through at the Donovan," Percival muttered, shame creeping into his heart.

"Oli," Dom said. Dom never addressed him as Oli, unless when he had something really awful to tell him.

"She left," Dom muttered, glancing at him nervously.

"What do you mean?" Percival inquired, frightened.

"No, Percival, Nell is not at Donovan's. Felix witnessed Addie confronting Nell, and when she was contacted, no one could locate her; her belongings were also missing. She vanished," Dom stated.

Percival sat, contemplating the new knowledge. Nell's face flashed before him, bringing with her the terror of the unknown. She was terrified to step into the outer world even with him at her side, and now she was alone someplace. He was afraid for her.

He felt a strong need to pursue her, locate her, and never let go. The orphanage flashed across his head; if she had to travel anyplace, she would first see her guardians. Percival rose up quickly from the table and made his way to the door, yelling instructions to get his carriage ready, unaware that his whole family was clamoring for him.

He was taken aback when he saw the King's guard approaching his door as he entered the foyer. He then observed his parents' apprehensive expressions and his brother's irate one.

The unexpected appearance of two King's guards seemed ominous. Lord Whitworth stepped ahead of everyone, concealing his family behind him. Percival was standing just behind him, and when he recognized the guards, he became nervous. They were in the Crown Prince's service, and given how he had left things with him, this was not going to end well.

"My Lord," The elder, heavier guard added, "I hope you're doing well. We're here on behalf of the Crown Prince, who has called Lord Percival Whitworth to the palace at this very moment."

"What is the meaning of this? A summons!" Lord Whitworth raised his voice. "Does the Prince not know what is the meaning of the summon?"

"We are only following orders, my Lord," The youngest of them expressed some fear.

"What is the summon for?" Lord Whitworth inquired, looking at both of them.

"We are unaware of the nature of the transaction, my Lord, but a number of letters were addressed to his Lordship demanding his attendance at the palace. The summons was issued when all of them remain unanswered and Lord Percival failed to show himself." The elder guard replied calmly.

"Father," Percival interrupted before Lord Whitworth could berate them or him anymore.

"Please, let the Prince know I am currently handling another business and will present myself once it is finished," Percival said the members of the guards.

"Go ahead to the palace and let the Prince know Lord Percival will be in the palace today itself and make sure to tell him he will be hearing from me," Lord Whitworth told them as they left.

"Percival, in my study now," Lord Whitworth strode away, allowing his children to follow.

Percival attempted to explain after everyone had entered the room, but Lord Whitworth interrupted him. The stillness fell over the study, and everyone knew better than to say out.

Lord Whitworth once had control over the King's guard when he had to knock on the door of rebels conspiring against the crown and plotting the King's death. He was most disturbed throughout his life by heading an army that seized many people's homes because of the selfish desire of a few individuals.

"Both of you have crossed a boundary," Lord Whitworth said, his voice full of force and authority. "Both of you should remember that your friendship does not come before the crown and its nobility. Now, you better have done something so heinous that the Prince sends the King's guard to my door, or by God's grace, I shall send both of you to the north in the winter to freeze."

"I was neglecting my duty for the preparation of the Prince's ball," Percival muttered, his head down.

"You cannot say no to summon, darling," Lady Whitworth spoke for the first time. "It is treason."

"What else?" Lord Whitworth inquired, "The Prince is angry with you over something; otherwise, he knows better than to send the King's guard."

"He believes the Princess is in love with me," Percival stated quietly.

He glanced up to see everyone's stupefied expression.

"How did you manage to do that?" Tavi spoke out, unable to contain his curiosity: "I am starting to think you have very bad luck with women."

"Octavian," Lady Seraphina silenced him, "This is not a laughing affair. Tell me, Percival, that you assured the Prince that it was not true."

"I can't. He was avoiding me, and then I became sidetracked by other things," Percival stated, taking a seat on the closest couch, exhausted of everything.

"By other things concerning Nell," Cedric said sternly.

"Yes," Percival said, "And I am going to go look for her now."

"No, you're not. You are going to the palace," Lord Whitworth replied with determination, "To settle this disagreement between the Prince and you."

"But, father," Percival said, "She needs me. You have no idea how terrified she is of the world; I need to locate her."

Lord Whitworth remained stubborn.

"Please, I just need to know whether she is safe. I swear to do anything you want, but just let me know she is safe," he implored.

"I am sorry, son," Lord Whitworth remarked gently, moved by his son's plight.

"I'll find her," Tavi said, stunning everyone. "Dom and I will go search for her. You should go to the palace; we'll locate her."

Percival's argument was stopped short by a tap at the door. Their butler told them that there was a severely wounded guy on the point of passing out who requested to see Lord Percival. Everyone proceeded to the parlor, and as predicted, the guy was bleeding through his bandaged head and hobbling on his feet. His face was unrecognizable behind the bruising.

"Percival Whitworth, are you Percival Whitworth?" The guy inquired through his anguish, staring through his blackened eye.

"Yes, who..."

"They took her, they took Nell."

23

Chapter Twenty-three

She was chained and gagged. There was agony and confusion, but not inside her. She didn't feel the anguish penetrate her spirit; despite her greatest dread coming true in front of her eyes, there was no pandemonium inside. She felt everything from the outside, as if her body was experiencing anguish, but she was completely numb on the inside.

She was not terrified; she was tranquil, and she felt as if these were her final moments of complete bliss. She longed to shut her eyes and go into the darkness. The darkness reminded her of the obsidian eyes. She should plunge into this abyss in the hopes of regaining those fearless eyes and loving lips.

How she yearned to spend her final moments in his embrace. She prayed she could have one more magnificent dance with him, or just a final look, and she would gladly leave this world.

The carriage rocked, reintroducing her spirit into her body, and she yelled out in anguish. She could now feel the leering and mocking laughs, as well as the repulsed touches. Soon, her senses were thrown off, the dread freezing her and rendering her unable to interpret her surroundings. She couldn't make out the sounds or comprehend anything. She felt a horrible breath at her neck, a voice that sent shivers up her spine, and the words that would haunt her life with nightmares: "I will come for you."

The anxiety grabbed her so tightly that she couldn't recall what occurred next. She awoke on a nice bed, staring up at the adorned ceiling with many stars. She wondered whether they shone in the dark. Her hand was bandaged, her face was burning slowly, and the ache in her back and legs became apparent as she regained consciousness.

Where was she? There was no one around. She attempted to sit up in bed with one hand, and the water bowl on the table toppled with a loud clang as a result of her actions. There was movement outside the door, and she waited with bated breath.

After what seemed like an eternity, a little girl around fifteen entered the room with a tray of food. She helped Nell sit up and set the tray on her lap without looking at her or saying anything.

"Where am I?" Nell questioned the girl quietly.

"Eat," she said monotonously, sitting in the furthest corner.

"Please, tell me where I am!" Nell begged once again, but her pleadings were unheard. She ate the soup and bread in silence, defeated.

The girl cleaned the tray and started changing the bandages and applying ointment to her injuries.

"What is your name?" Nell inquired, hoping to encourage the girl to speak, but was greeted with stony stillness.

"My name is Nell," she began with a grin, waiting for the response. She felt as if she were speaking to a stone statue.

"The broth was good, thank you," she said again.

"Don't talk," the girl said as Nell opened her lips to speak again.

"Why not?" Nell inquired curiously.

"I will be punished, I can't talk, so be silent," the girl muttered gently while putting ointment on her face.

Nell stopped her mouth after that. She gazed around the room, which was neat and modestly furnished. There was no glass, and she observed that the door had no bolt from the inside. She was in a box and began to feel smothered.

"Drink," the girl murmured, raising the drink to her nose.

"What is it?" Nell inquired suspiciously.

"Medicine, drink," the girl pleaded.

Nell unwillingly put the liquid in her lips; it smelt delicious and tasted like honey. She swallowed it down greedily, enjoying the flavor.

"Sleep," the girl instructed. Nell did not want to sleep; she wanted to know where she was and why. But soon she realized the chamber was spinning; she attempted to move but couldn't, and a soft hand guided her back to sleep.

She realized she was being drugged and that she was in a perilous situation before darkness overtook her.

The next time she woke up, the ceiling had the same stars, and she wondered whether they would shine in the dark. She sat up immediately, terror setting in, and looked about for a way out.

"There's no way out, the only way in."

Nell looked for the speaker and saw a woman reclining on a nice sofa, drinking tea. She seemed wealthy based on her appearance and attire. Her demeanor exuded grandeur, yet something was off. Nell's instincts told her not to trust her.

"Who are you?" Nell asked in a raspy voice.

"You can call me Madame," the lady murmured, setting her cup down.

"What is this place? Why am I here?" Nell questioned whether her anger was obvious.

"Shh, darling," the lady whispered while approaching towards her. "You have so many questions. Oh, and that fire in your eyes, you're going to make me a fortune."

The lady grabbed hold of Nell's face and examined it from side to side.

"Hmm, magical medication works again. The scars are fading nicely," the lady added, smiling to herself.

"What is this place?" Nell questioned forcefully, breaking away from the woman's grip.

"Ah!" She moaned as she perched on the side of the bed. "This place! Some call it paradise, others hell, but it only has room for abandoned and unloved beauties like you."

"I want to leave," Nell said vehemently.

"There's no 'I' for you. Do you realize how pricey you are?" The lady stated it tauntingly.

"What do you mean?" Nell asked, her voice trembling.

"Oh, naive girl. Tell me: have you ever been touched before?" The Madame inquired casually.

"What is this place? Why am I here? I need to go. I have to go," Nell whispered, attempting to stand but unable to feel her hands or legs.

"What did you do to me?" She inquired with wide eyes.

"A sweet potion to keep you compliant," Madame said. "Now, I offer you all the luxury if you do what I ask. You're very fortunate that those guys brought you here. You will only have to serve Lords and Nobility, not filthy commoners."

"I'd rather kill myself than whore myself out," Nell muttered, appalled.

Madame laughed aloud.

"Oh, poor girl. Whore?! You are not a whore, but a lover." Madame stated with an eerie smirk on her face that she was a lover to various guys every night.

Nell merely looked at her with venom in her eyes. She told herself that she would sooner die than set foot in an institution like this, and she will keep that pledge the first opportunity she gets.

"Feisty! If you continue doing this, you will experience discomfort." Madame remarked menacingly before reverting back into her cheerful self, "I will try to find someone who will go easy on you for the first time, of course, and who can pay for your exorbitant fee." The Madame stated before tapping on the door with her beautiful fingers, "Next time I visit, you better be prepared, or you won't remember your first time."

The door quickly opened, and she saw a big guy standing outside before it was closed again. She was left alone, and she needed to devise a way to leave this jail of her life before it was too late.

Nell was kept drugged and incapable of thinking. She didn't know how many days had gone or what time of day it was. She was losing her sanity, and every day she became more anxious to go. She craved human interaction with someone other than the girl who brought her meals but didn't speak.

She attempted to commit suicide by starving herself and refusing to eat, but the girl forced her to eat, leaving her powerless and her head foggy. Every passing instant, she thought that anything would be preferable to this pain.

She begged the girl to tell Madame; she would do everything she asked, but she couldn't see those walls any longer; the isolation was twisting her mind against her.

She waited patiently, realizing she was more alert than usual. They must have reduced the potion dosages.

"I'm glad you came around," Madame said. Nell understood not to stare if she wanted to remain awake and discover an escape route.

"His Lordship is here, Madame," the soldier outside remarked in a harsh tone.

Madame swooned when the lovely Lord entered the room behind her. "My Lord, I hope you will love the new addition to our squadron," she said.

Nell stared at the guy standing in front of her, shocked.

"I do!" He replied, grinning.

24

Chapter Twenty-four

Nell's intellect was clear, but her body remained feeble. She was aided in joining the Lord and Madame for a supper immediately across from her bedroom. Without her strength, she chose to investigate her surroundings and remember them, but she couldn't see very well in the dim hallway.

His Lordship and the Madame were sat quite next to each other, with just a hairbreadth separating them. They didn't notice she was sitting in front of them, still engrossed in their world. He appeared heavenly, looking at Madame with affection in his eyes, and the tip of her ears was tinted with scarlet. They seem nearly in love.

Nell was taken aback by the spectacle in front of her, wondering how two individuals of such different social status could be so obviously in love. He was a Lord, and she oversaw this abhorrent institution. She and Percival had little possibility of ever being together. However, when she looked at the pair in front of her, she realized how vastly different their circumstances were.

In front of her were individuals who knew exactly what their futures will be yet were not frightened to love one another. Nell knew her condition had improved significantly, and a solitary glimmer of hope entered her heart.

She was so frightened of being harmed that she didn't even give herself the wherewithal to enjoy a happy life as long as it lasted. Life was full of ups and downs, but her fear of falling prevented her from enjoying it, and she realized she hadn't lived at all. She lived in this world but did not really live, except for those little times with Percival.

She wanted more, to be with Percival, to be alive.

"Why do you want her?" Nell overheard Madame remark after the lunch, "You don't like naive, virgin women."

Nell was outraged that the lady was so openly informing him about her, even if it was a common practice at the institution.

"Then what do I like?" He asked seductively, looking into her eyes.

"Someone experienced and experimental," Madame said seductively. "I can show you what you like."

Nell coughed repeatedly, clearly uncomfortable with their discourse. The pair looked at Nell for the first time but said nothing.

"She is so untamed," Madame replied, dissatisfied. "I have other beautiful girls I can show you."

"She is perfect, I assure you," The Lord kissed Madame's hand, making her fluster even more.

He really was a charmer.

"You still haven't told me, why do you want her?" Madame questioned, pouting, and she seemed innocent for a time, but Nell knew she wasn't.

"She is a gift," The Lord murmured, looking at Nell. Nell could not make anything of him.

He was like an enigma; she wasn't sure whether he was there to assist or undermine her.

The table had been cleared, but they were still sitting. Nobody said anything for a long time.

"Is there any chance she will be back here in the future?" The Madame inquired, gazing across at Nell.

Nell maintained her composure despite the fact that the rebuke was on the tip of her tongue. Even if she had the worst nightmare, she would never return here.

"I don't believe so," he said, sipping on his wine.

"You do know she cost me a fortune," The Madame said, her business mask back on her face, all of her swooning and flushing gone at once.

Nell was not surprised by the shift in her demeanor; she pondered how many faces this lady had and which one was her genuine personality. She gazed at him with no affection in her eyes.

"And I will pay ten times that," he added, still pleasant, but something seemed odd. He stared at her as if she were simply another lady, rather than the one he had been staring at with such passion moments before.

Nell had always known that people were deceptive, but seeing it in action made her furious.

"Not enough, my Lord," Madame said. "Do you realize how much money I could make from her? She is extraordinarily attractive and will be in great demand."

Nell saw his jaw clench as he placed his wine glass down.

"Ten times. And no one will ever talk of this again," He continued smugly, knowing full well that he was the ruler here, "And I will make certain that no damage comes to this location."

It was a clear threat, and the Madame knew better than to confront him. For the ton, he was London's most charming bachelor, a legendary rakehell whose grin could melt you. But Madame knew he had a vicious streak that would come out when provoked. He was friendlier than everyone else, yet it was unwise to disregard his desires.

Madame signaled to take Nell away and prepare her. Nell observed their conversation, overwhelmed with trepidation. She saw a new side of him today, which scared her. She worried whether she'd wind up somewhere worse than here.

She proceeded to a dark hallway with dimly lit lamps lighting the path. Except for the rustle of their robes and the sound of their slippers striking the ground, there was silence.

She felt liberated as she was led out via a little door to a lone carriage parked in the distance. As soon as she returned to her seat in front of him, the carriage began to move.

The stillness persisted as she observed him, trying to figure out what was going on in his head.

"What day is it?" she said.

"Pardon," he murmured with amazement.

"I was kept sedated all the time, I do not know how long I was kept imprisoned," she claimed.

She observed him balling his fist and wondered whether she shouldn't have said anything. But she felt bewildered and lost, and she wanted to know.

"It's been 5 days since your capture," He said, relaxed.

"It feels like an eternity," she muttered. She couldn't believe she'd lost her mind that quickly.

"It must have been torturous," he remarked.

"When there is nothing but emptiness around you, your mind starts to play tricks on you," she added, trembling at the memories.

"How do you know? How did you find me?" Nell inquired curiously.

"Hector came to the manor injured and bleeding, demanding to meet Percival," he said.

Percival! An odd sensation flooded over her, and her heart began to beat a bit quicker. She wanted to inquire about him, but she stopped. She had no idea what the guy sitting in front of her was up to, and she would be foolish to blindly trust him. She just wanted to meet him once, and a peek was enough. Is it a fairy tale if his Lordship takes her to Percival?

"Where are you taking me?" She asked.

"Somewhere I do not want to take you, but I don't have a choice," he said.

Nell didn't know what to make of his response; he could see the fear on her face.

"Home. I'm taking you to Whitworth manor," he said quickly to calm her.

The response should have made her pleased, but instead it made her worried. She had no idea what awaited her at the Whitworth mansion. She sat guarded, unable to trust the guy in front of her.

"If it were up to me, I would never take you to my house," he said, as if he could read her thoughts. There was so much wrong with her coming to Whitworth Manor, but her heart refused to listen.

"I do not care about anything or anyone in this world other than my family," He added, his eyes flashing and that gorgeous grin remaining on his face, "And the only reason I am doing this is that my brother is going insane with worry for you."

"I suggest you think twice before doing anything that will hurt him," he added, his expression harsh and menacing, before returning to his normal jovial self.

Nell swallowed; she had seen Whitworth might and authority in action for the first time, and now she may confront more than one of them.

She got out of the carriage in front of the entrance of Whitworth Manor, nervous about what lay within.

She turned around to see him eagerly waiting to lead her inside.

"Lord Octavian, thank you for saving me from that hell," she whispered gratefully, tears in her eyes.

25

Chapter Twenty-five

Percival has been tirelessly looking for Nell for the last several days. When Hector arrived to Whitworth Manor, battered and injured, he passed out before he could say anything further.

The doctor was summoned, and when he returned to his senses, Percival discovered that the Orphanage had been assaulted around midnight. Hector battled them until he lost consciousness. When he awoke in the morning, Mr. Davies informed him that those guys were from Donovan County and had previously attacked their orphanage for Nell many years before. They weren't sure what to do next? What is the best way to locate and aid her?

An elderly man on the verge of death and a young guy struggling to stand upright could only depend on the kindness of the stronger.

Mr. Davies persuaded Hector to travel to Whitworth Manor and beg Lord Percival, since he was their final chance for finding Nell.

Percival was in the jostling carriage on his journey back to London from Donovan, where his hunt for Nell had failed. The guys who left Donovan County and must have stolen her were most likely still in London, which meant she was still in their possession.

A shred of hope that she was still alive, along with the foul dark sense of her state during the capture, continued building up within him, and it became harder to breathe with each passing second. He couldn't let hope die, couldn't allow the last shred of rationality slip away.

They believe that throughout the disaster, we not only knew our genuine friends, but also our true family.

He gazed up at Dom's sleeping body in front of him, and he realized that even if he lost himself totally, he would never be alone. He was astonished when Octavian offered to file a complaint with Scotland Yard, and Cedric told him, grudgingly but on his own initiative, that he would speak with Mr. Davies and everyone at the orphanage to find out as much as he could.

He prayed that they were more successful than he was.

Percival arrived to the Whitworth mansion about noon and found everyone at the luncheon table together; he was astounded that his family could sit so peacefully when his life was falling apart around him. Did they not realize what he was going through? How significant was she to him? How could they?

And then he realized that he had denied her for so long because of their social status; how could he expect his brother, who had never been in love, to understand him, or his parents, whose legacy was now jeopardized as a result of his recklessness?

"Have you found her? Where is Scotland Yard with its investigation? Has anyone found anything? She needs to be in London." He questioned anxiously, stopping when everyone remained quiet. "What's wrong?"

"Not a word," His mother urged, putting her hand up to quiet all the lips that opened to remark on Percival's condition. "I don't want any of you to say something and make this all worse."

"Ma," Percival muttered, afraid.

"We haven't found anything yet, darling," She stated calmly, "The search is still ongoing, but we need to take a break so that we can restart. Tavi is seeing an officer from Scotland Yard after lunch, and I am certain we will locate her shortly. Now, I'll prepare your bath, so you can regain your wits."

Percival nodded and said, "When will the officer arrive?"

"Uh," Tavi began, "He's not. I'm going to meet him."

"Why?" Dom questioned, his voice weary, "We never go to Scotland Yard, they come to the manor."

"Tavi has already agreed on the meeting," Cedric said, adding, "You two must be tired, let them proceed as they have decided."

"Who is this officer? I have a friend in..." Dom said, his eyes drooping.

"You don't know him," Tavi quickly interrupted, surprising everyone.

"Tavi," Percival said cautiously, "What are you hiding?"

"Nothing, brother," Tavi said. "Why?"

"Because you are a horrible liar, my son," Lord Whitworth replied from the head of the table.

"There has been no complaint made with Scotland Yard. They have no idea about this," Cedric stated callously while Tavi remained mute.

"What do you mean?" Dom remarked, "I'm suddenly alive."

"Octavian Leopold Whitworth, what is the meaning of this?" His mother yelled, and Percival was certain he was having a terrible nightmare and would soon awaken to a better reality.

Everyone remained silently, their gazes fixed on Tavi, who was nervously twitching under their gazes.

"I asked him not to involve Scotland Yard," Cedric calmly said. "We are more than capable enough to handle this on our own, we should not present an opportunity for others to go digging and throw dirt at us the first chance they get."

Percival could not hear his mother berating Cedric, nor did he feel himself wandering away from everyone. He locked the door to his room, feeling all of his power leave him, sliding down the door, wanting to scream in anguish.

The darkness was sucking him up, and he could hear her screaming, sobbing, and pleading. He felt deceived and enraged, and he didn't realize he was crying into his own arms.

He heard banging on his door and Dom's voice telling him to open it or he'd smash it down. Percival wanted to shout at him to leave him alone, but he couldn't get the words out. He hesitantly opened the door for Dom.

"Percival, you can't give up," Dom urged, interrupting his words to glance at his elder brother's tear-filled face.

Dom stopped for a long time, trying to think of the appropriate words to say.

"Did you... did you know that too?" Percival inquired, his voice croaking.

"No, I cannot think Tavi lied to me. But we can't give up now," Dom said quietly.

"What if we are too late?" Percival asked, dejected.

"What if we are not?" Dom inquired with optimism.

Dom was correct. What if she was safe someplace and biding her time? She had kept herself safe all these years, so he had to think she found a way to survive.

Percival noticed how fatigued his body was as he lowered himself into the bathtub, despite the fact that his heart and mind could not stop thinking about her, he stopped himself from going further into those ideas; he needed to think she was safe and that he would rescue her in time.

Percival waited for Dom in the parlor, and a carriage was already waiting for them outside. Dom ran in, apologizing for being late. They glanced up to find Cedric standing at the entrance, arms crossed, waging a silent fight between them.

"You have made up your mind, haven't you?" Cedric inquired in a frigid tone that he only reserved for his parliamentarian opponents.

"I have, and you can't stop me," Percival said with similar enthusiasm.

Dom was relieved his parents were not around to see what had become of their children at this point.

"Do you even understand all that you are risking?" Cedric inquired, agitated. "We don't know who the snakes in sheep's clothing are who will join and further feed the uproar caused by our one error. You know better than anybody how deceitful all those nobilities are who are afraid of our authority but would stop at nothing to pull us down."

"I understand, Cedric," Percival said fiercely. "What is the worst thing that could happen to us? Our reputation will be ruined, but her destiny will be worse than death."

Cedric took a long breath before declaring.

"I won't let you leave and risk everything."

26

Chapter Twenty-six

Nell went behind Octavian down the main corridor. The grandeur and opulence of the Whitworth mansion would have stopped her in her tracks if not for her dread of the unknown. She remained at the Whitworth house, but she never ventured out of the service corridors or her apartments.

Now, as she traveled the halls that could only be described as being from a dream realm, her heart hammered in her chest and her breathing staggered with each step. She could hear the rising voices of angry and irritated people speaking. She remained transfixed, protected by Tavi from the gaze of the folks standing on the other side of the door.

"What is going on here?" She heard Octavian inquire as her gaze remained fixated on the back of his head.

"Tavi, finally," Someone spoke with relief.

She saw Tavi shaking his head in approval when no question was posed. He must have understood the person in the parlor, and she took a step back, anxiety creeping into her heart.

"You took your sweet time; I was running out of things to argue about with Percival," the same individual added, relieved.

She lowered her gaze to her feet at hearing Percival's name. He was right there on the other side of the door, yet he felt far away. She came here to follow her heart, but now it was tingling with expectation.

Did he love her as much as she loved him? Or did he see her as simply another woman? Or worse, a transitory fancy? But before she could take another step back, she heard him beckon her.

"Nell?"

She could only see his hazy visage through her teary eyes.

"It's you?" he said breathlessly. She could only nod briefly, unable to swallow the knot in her throat.

He began approaching toward her, and she could feel everyone's attention on them. When he approached to bring her into his arms, she recoiled from his contact and looked down at the floor. He took her hands in his, and she wriggled them out, tightening them in her skirt.

Percival couldn't understand why she was pulling away from him, so he attempted to make her look at him, but her gaze wandered about the others in the room, revealing how uncomfortable she was.

"Come," Percival murmured, taking her hand, "Let's go to my chamber."

She stood motionless, her eyes wide open, starring at the Whitworth parents and the boys, who were peering at them. She made her way to the Whitworth estate, but she would never be accepted here, no matter how much Percival loved her. Lord Whitworth confirmed it.

Lord Whitworth remarked, "Percival, take her to your estate," and walked away with his wife.

"Dom, call for the carriage," Cedric said, as Tavi and he followed their parents.

Nell knew she would never be welcomed anywhere, but rejection hurt her heart. But there was a silver lining: Percival was still on her side, somehow.

Was she removing him from his family? She would explore into this later, realizing it was not a part of her delusion but rather fact.

Percival made no effort to touch her; he maintained his distance, which she appreciated. She boarded the carriage and kept her gaze averted throughout the trip.

"My Lord," Mr. Fitzgerald welcomed them as they entered his land. He stared at Nell on Percival's side, a million thoughts racing through his mind, but remained silent.

"Mr. Fitzgerald, please send for a doctor and order a bath to be drawn at once in my chamber for Nell," Percival told him, "And send someone to help her."

Percival led Nell to his bedroom and seated her in front of the fireplace. The cold and darkness outside were increasing, and the fire in the hearth provided much-needed warmth. He handed her a glass of wine, which she quickly drank.

"Slowly," Percival murmured.

She had yet to say another word or even glance at him. She wanted to keep living this wonderful dream as long as she could with him at her side. She was afraid he'd disappear into thin air before she could fill her eyes with his face.

Nell didn't feel like herself; everything around her was fuzzy, and her mind began to whirl. She worried that the medicine she was compelled to take had permanently transformed her. She saw his obsidian eyes widen with anxiety before darkness seized them.

Nell had a dream she went back in time when she first met Percival. She was looking after him and chatting to him while he was disoriented in his sleep. However, the roles were now flipped. She was the one in his position, her eyesight blurred and unable to see anything in the dark.

She was resting behind a pile of blankets. Her hand gripped in a warm one, and his voice whispered lovely nothings into her ear. And what a wonderful dream it was to hear him utter what she had wanted to say for so long but never had the confidence to express before slipping back into the darkness.

"I love you," The last words Nell heard.

Nell felt a little better the following day, and the doctor stated she would be entirely recovered in two days. She questioned if she would really recover. Physical wounds may be healed, but mental wounds will always bleed.

Percival remained away from her, only appearing when the doctor came to check on her. Sophia and Eleanor, who took turns taking care of her, refused to talk to her; she could sense they were upset with her.

And who wouldn't be? She was striving for the heavens when she hardly deserved the moon.

She decided to go once she was fit to travel. If necessary, she would go far away, even to the end of the globe. Nobody could harm her there anymore.

On the third day, the doctor advised her to go for a stroll in the garden, and she would soon be back to her normal self. The doctor informed Percival, sternly, that he no longer needed to visit his estate for Nell; she would gradually regain her vigor.

Percival and Nell made their way to the garden, strolling side by side without glancing at one other. They strolled, troubled by the quiet surrounding them, waiting for each other to speak first. Nell mustered the bravery as they sat down at the table, breakfast ready for them.

"My Lord," Nell murmured gently. "Thank you for everything. I apologize for causing you a great deal of trouble."

"Nell," Percival groaned. Nell stared up at the side of his face as he remained silent after saying her name. He was fixated on the green vine growing gradually up the side of his estate wall.

He groaned again, and his gaze fell to his feet, unknowing that she was examining him and filling him in her heart.

"I was afraid," Percival spoke slowly and calmly. "I believed I had lost you, and I had never been so terrified in my life. And then you approached me when I was half mad. But you didn't want me, and my heart crushed. Perhaps in another existence, you will accept me. But even if you don't, you're the only one I adore in this one."

Percival turned to find Nell already staring at him, tears flowing down her cheeks and her lips trembling. And, despite every nerve in his body wanting to soothe her, he held himself back from doing anything she didn't want, leaving him with just three words that could express all he felt.

"I love you," he said.

27

Chapter Twenty-seven

Percival was crying in front of the lady he loved, unable to do anything. He didn't understand why she was sobbing, and he feared the worst.

But he couldn't keep his sentiments within. He needed to express out loud that he loved her, regardless of how she felt about him. He lost her once because he let her go lightly. This time, however, things would be different. He was going to protect her and, if she let it, show her all of his love.

If she does not return his love, he will provide her safety and care, and he will love her from afar. But he will never again let her walk out into the terrible world alone. He couldn't handle the notion of what may happen to her. He never wanted to experience the terrible worry of not knowing her safety. He pledged that he would do all in his power to ensure that no one touched her.

"Do not weep, Nell," He replied, brushing away her tears. "I will not put my emotions on you. I just wanted to tell you before my heart bursts. You are not required to reciprocate."

He watched her hands reach up to his palms, which were still caressing her face. He prepared himself for rejection, but was astonished when she clasped his hands in hers and attempted to bury her face in them, weeping even harder.

He carefully untangled his hands from hers and hugged her, keeping her close as she wailed against his chest. She had been strong for so long, and he was glad she trusted him enough to let go of herself in front of him.

He heard her whisper but couldn't understand what she was saying, but he wanted to hear all she said. He softly murmured her name into her ear and felt a shudder go through her body.

"Nell," he said, "I can't hear you, love?" The endearment slipped out of his lips before he could stop himself.

Nell glanced up and quickly but boldly mashed her lips on his.

Percival's heart stopped racing, and he sat motionless like a statue as she attempted to kiss him. When he didn't answer, she drew away, tears streaming down her cheeks.

Percival snapped out of his daze as her perplexed expression crossed his thoughts. She kissed him, and he, like a fool, could not reply. Her gushing tears terrified him; he knew he had to act quickly before she began to have bad thoughts.

The only thing he could think of at the time was to kiss her with all his being, and that's exactly what he did until both of them pulled apart, gasping for breath. There was the intensity they had always felt when they touched, but this time something else was there, which worried and intrigued them at the same time.

"Excuse me; I was simply startled. I never imagined you would ever kiss me. I was sure you would reject me. Does this mean you accept me?" he said, her face flushed.

She nodded and looked away sheepishly.

"Do you love me?" He inquired genuinely, holding his heart in his palm, knowing full well that she had the ability to crush it under her feet.

"I already answered it. It is not my fault you did not hear it," she teased him.

"Nell," Percival said, "This is not fair."

Percival laughed at her arrogant tear-stained face. The tension in the air subsided, and he felt everything would be OK now. There was a long way to go, but they were certain they would make it.

For the following two days, Percival remained at her side. The more he was in her company, the more he desired her. They were sat in the parlor, and the stillness enveloped them in pleasant warmth.

"My Lord," Mr. Fitzgerald entered the salon, holding a letter titled "Letter from the Palace."

Percival muttered behind his breath. He had entirely forgotten about the outer world since the day he discovered Nell. He was enveloped in her and did not want to get out.

"Is everything alright?" Nell questioned as he read the letter.

"Well, the Princess sent the subtle threat of executing me," Percival replied, grinning.

Nell didn't find it funny and glanced at him blankly, silently seeking an explanation.

"I was supposed to help the Princess prepare for the ball," he remarked hesitantly.

Nell opened and closed her lips, unsure what to say. Percival held her hand in his, calming her fears.

"It is not because of you," he murmured, startling her.

He laughed, knowing that she would have chastised herself for keeping him away from his duties. However, she didn't. He was the one who never wanted to be apart from her. He was scared she'd disappear in thin air if he allowed her a moment to return to the darkness in her head.

"I will be here," she said, surprising Percival. It was lovely how they knew in an instant to reassure one other.

"You should visit the palace and help the Princess," Squeezing his hand, she whispered, "I will be here when you come back."

Percival leaned forward and pressed his forehead on hers.

"Do you promise?"

"I promise."

Percival was terrified. She was still shaken, and he did not want to go. But he couldn't disregard his responsibilities any longer. He was still neglecting his family, and when the time came, he would have to face them too.

Percival left the mansion hesitantly, hoping that Nell would still be there when he returned. Drowned in Nell's thoughts, it wasn't until he reached the palace doors that he understood the little mistake he left unsolved had grown into a massive monster.

He thought it was better to tackle the situation straight on than to let it develop any further. He went to the Prince's room, but as predicted, the Prince did not greet him. He was about to burst in when he heard the Princess summon him.

"My Lord," she replied, unable to hide her joy at seeing him again, but quickly concealing it.

"This is completely unacceptable, my Lord," she sniffed mockingly. "Are you going to break your promise?"

"Your Highness," Percival bowed politely, "I apologize for my actions. I'm here to make good on my promise. I wanted to see the Prince before starting the preparations."

"You will be wasting your time, my Lord," she added, yelling so her voice could be heard through the room walls. "He is sulking like a child for the utterly stupid thing."

"He's in there," Percival murmured to the Princess, despite the fact that the guards in the Prince's room showed no signs of their master's presence.

"Yes," she said. "For days. He hardly left his room. God knows what he's doing. Let us leave him to his own devices for the time being. We'll deal with him later."

Percival left his buddy alone for now and spent the whole day with the Princess. To his great astonishment, Princess had done more than half of the preparation perfectly, and she clearly understood what she was doing.

"I used to be in charge of the Christmas ball back home," she said, seeing his awe at what she had achieved on her own.

"I have ordered for your chambers to be ready, my Lord," She said with a smile, "We have a big day tomorrow."

"I will be returning to my estate tonight, your highness," Percival remarked, adding, "I assure you I will be here at the break of the dawn."

"Why? Is it due to the rumors that have been circulating?" She asked openly.

"I have someone waiting at home," he said simply.

The possibility of seeing Nell again filled him with a sense of pleasure. The mansion was quiet, and panic began to grip him. He hurried out, two steps at a time, and came to a halt in front of Nell's room.

Nothing. He could not hear anything.

He unlocked the door with shaky fingers and breathed a sigh of relief when he saw Nell asleep. His sleepy body pulled him to her, and without thinking, he crawled beneath the blankets, embracing her in his arms and muttering, before falling asleep.

"Thank you for staying."

28

Chapter Twenty-eight

Nell could not sleep. She waited for him to return, and when he did, she claimed she was sleeping. She was scared he'd hear her pulse pounding so hard in her chest as he sought solace in her after a tough day. It gave her a weird sensation.

Isn't this how married couples live? Reluctantly leaving the other in the morning, spending the day yearning for the other to return, and falling asleep in each other's arms at night. Nell felt like her heart was about to explode out of her chest at the prospect. She felt it would be presumptuous of her to consider marriage.

She has been in the seventh sky since he proclaimed his love. She nearly thought she had died and gone to paradise if it hadn't been for the cold shoulder from the other occupants of the estate.

Percival fussed over her every moment of the day, and she soaked in the sensation of being adored. Her heart remained guarded, and his love continued to worry her, but she told her heart to relax and enjoy the delight. Nothing was permanent, and she didn't want to live with the consequences of allowing her fear to govern her.

Nell was startled when everyone in the home began to be friends with her again. But now that she was their master's sweetheart, anybody who harbored ill will against her would keep it hidden and put up a good show in order to avoid her wrath. It was the way of life, and it bothered her.

She wanted Sophia and Eleanor to be her pals again, and Mrs. Fitzgerald would let her be a nuisance in the kitchen. Maybe it was time she attempted to befriend them again; she wasn't fearful of people's motives anymore since she felt comfortable with him by her side. She felt courageous enough to take the first step.

After Percival departed for the palace in the morning, she went to see Mrs. Fitzgerald, who was preparing something delicious as usual in the kitchen. When she saw Nell come, she flinched slightly, not expecting her.

"Mrs. Fitzgerald," Nell replied, taking the lady out of her anguish. "I need to speak to you."

Sophia and Eleanor arrived from the side entrance just as expected. Nell realized it was lunchtime after all, and she had arrived at the incorrect time. Instead of turning away, she sat at the table as everyone stared at her.

"Do you need anything?" Sophia questioned, hardly containing her displeasure.

"Yes, I thought I'd join you for lunch like we used to," Nell replied, smiling despite feeling like she was infringing on their space. Their eyes bulged out at her words, and she couldn't stop laughing.

"Now, girls, stop staring and get the plates," she heard Mrs. Fitzgerald say.

There were no words uttered, only the gentle clatter of silverware as everyone filled their plates. This was not how Nell intended things to be; every minute she felt out of place, as she had her whole life.

"Are you feeling well now?" Mrs. Fitzgerald inquired, and her comments immediately relaxed Nell.

"Yes, I am well now, thank you," she said nervously.

"Why are you playing with your food then?" Mr. Fitzgerald requested reprimanding. "Eat, before it gets cold."

Nell's face broke into the brightest grin, and Mrs. Fitzgerald's lips curved into a smile at her, a subtle understanding going between them.

"We are sorry, Nell," Mrs. Fitzgerald began, resting her hand on Nell's across the table. "We came across as a little rude to you. But we had no idea which one was the real you, and we felt deceived. We had to be on our watch, but when you arrived to join us today, I knew you were the Nell we know."

Nell's eyes welled up with tears as she reflected on the easy acceptance, but she was being brave and attempting to push her luck a little further.

"I did not tell you everything about myself. I let you think I was a simple maid from Donovan while I concealed the fact of my mother," Nell replied, embarrassed.

Something about her pals inspired her to open out about her feelings.

"You are not your mother, Nell," Sophia hurriedly said.

"You know," Nell answered, astonished. "How?"

"Lord Dominic has been visiting every day to check on his Lordship since the day you arrived," Mrs. Fitzgerald stated. "On days when his Lordship was not available to receive him, he inquired about both of you. He felt our unasked queries and described the whole situation."

"Now, don't be furious with him for revealing your secret. He just wanted us to be more understanding," Sophia grumbled.

"I will not," Nell responded, smiling. She was a little disturbed that Lord Dominic had informed them about her without her permission, but his motive was pure, and she felt comforted rather than angry.

"But I'm upset with myself because you couldn't trust me enough to share your secret," Eleanor added, her eyes downcast.

"I apologize, Eleanor. I never speak about it with anybody. I'm not sure I'll ever be able to," Nell whispered gently.

"But now you were going to if I hadn't interrupted you," Sophia remarked, perplexed.

"You are my only friends, and I wanted to be honest with you," Nell said genuinely. She saw the woman in front of them become noticeably softer.

Addie's face appeared before her eyes for a brief period. She urgently wanted to befriend Nell, and she worried whether she was alone in the gorgeous palace, surrounded by everyone.

"I hope we can stay friends like this forever," Nell stated cheerfully.

"I am sorry I was angry at you," Sophia replied regrettably. "Lord Percival never left your side even for a second while you were unconscious, and one day I discovered him whispering to you in your sleep. He asked whether you'd leave him when you woke up."

Nell was astonished. "How can you make him believe that?" Sophia complained.

"You were angry with me because you thought I will leave him," She spoke without thinking.

"Well, sure," Sophia conceded, "He is such a gentleman and loves you so much, plus he is from Whitworth. Why would you consider letting him go?

Nell rushed towards Sophia and held her passionately. "I won't," she told Sophia.

She spent the remainder of the day with them, and they never mentioned her mother or inquired about what happened to her.

Sophia and Eleanor mocked her hard as the evening approached, seeing her inadvertent glance toward the door every second. It was clear she was waiting for Percival.

She was ecstatic that her friendship had been renewed and was now laying in Percival's arms. She reflected about Sophia's remarks and wanted to rouse him awake and tell him that she loves him just as much as he loves her.

She focused on his face, memorizing every curve and shape. His obsidian eyes were so captivating that she could never look at him the same way again. His face felt like it was carved from a hard, cold stone, yet even in his slumber, he seemed soft and kind.

She nestled closer into his hug, buried her face in his chest and listening to his pulse. When she felt tired, she looked up, kissed the edge of his chin, and muttered.

"I love you too."

29

Chapter Twenty-nine

The following day, Nell was in the garden, attempting to learn all she could about the gorgeous flowers from the gardener. He was overjoyed that someone wanted to hear him talk about his knowledge of all the plants and herbs.

"Nell," she heard Sophia say, "Lord Dominic is here for you."

Nell pivoted quickly, her focus on the flowers all gone. Sophia curtsied to his Lordship, and she then exited.

"Miss Nell," he began, his green eyes flashing like the ones that startled her. "I hope I'm not interrupting you. I just came to check how you were doing.

"Milord, uh," Nell stammered.

The appearance of another Whitworth sibling seemed worrisome.

"I am fine, milord. Thank you," she said with a cautious grin.

"If it doesn't bother you, may we make some small talk? I have ordered tea to be served at the garden table," he added, hoping.

"Yes, milord," she responded, her mind racing with ideas. She could image all the threats he'd level at her while smiling like an angel.

Nell followed him as he led the way; the table was already set with a delicious breakfast. She wanted to laugh, but she couldn't say no to his offer.

"Please help yourself," he urged. "I am famished."

Nell didn't have much of an appetite, worrying about this Whitworth sibling and what he was capable of, while he ate breakfast like it was nothing.

"I am afraid I haven't introduced myself properly," he apologized. Was this a ploy? He introduced himself in an unconventional manner. A person of lower position gets presented to the one above them, and she was well aware of this regulation.

"I'm Dominic. I am Percival's youngest brother, and you can call me Dom," he stated with boyish enthusiasm.

Nell was taken aback; she had expected a lengthy number of titles that she would never remember, but instead he asked her to address him by his name. That would be ridiculous.

"I am Nell," Nell said, for lack of a better retort.

"It is finally nice to meet you, Nell," He replied cheerfully. "Can I call you Nell?"

"Yes, milord," she said, wondering of his intentions. It is usually the nicest folks that stab you in the back.

"I hope I am not making you uncomfortable," he continued, his tone tinged with fear.

"No, milord," she said.

"How are you feeling right now? Tavi informed us about how he discovered you." He inquired, "We took care of those bastards, they are going to rot in a cell for next decade to come."

"I am well, milord, and thank you," she said, focusing on his inquiry.

"How's Percival? It feels like I'm always late to catch him. I hope he is doing better now that he is visiting the palace." He hoped Nell would continue to open up.

"He is, uh, good," she said, unsure whether it was the correct thing to say.

"So, when are you planning to get married?" He inquired casually, but Nell became really concerned. Marriage to Percival Whitworth looked like a pleasant and innocent dream in the dead of night, but nothing could be farther from the truth.

"Oh, stupid me; has Percival not proposed to you yet? He's going to murder me for spoiling it." He said, terrified, "Can you pretend you didn't hear me say any of this?"

"Milord, I believe you are mistaken," Nell said. Lord Dominic was unlike his other brother. Despite the fact that their green eyes were the same, he had a certain purity.

"The ton wouldn't even accept me as his Lordship's mistress," she said frankly, for that was the truth.

Dominic departed after a short conversation, and she felt more apprehensive than ever. He informed her that Percival wanted to marry her and has made it obvious to his family. He was willing to battle his family for her. It didn't calm her anxieties when Dominic offered to be on their side, claiming that his parents would embrace them once they saw how happy Percival is with her.

But could she keep him happy forever? They may have forgotten about the world outside these four walls, but sooner or later they will have to confront it. Will he be able to confront them? She was well aware of how cruel the world can be; her innocence, her youth, and everything else had been ripped away from her.

Nell assisted Percival in preparing his favorite meal. She didn't know anything about the guy despite spending so many days with him. Every time they ate, there was something fresh on the table, and it was all for her, though she would pick up little items. He had a sweet taste, and Mrs. Fitzgerald had cooked a delicious meal for him.

Nell wasn't exactly an expert at creating a romantic atmosphere, and Percival was buried in his thoughts, hardly focusing on his dinner. They didn't say much throughout the dinner, but Nell realized she needed to do something to brighten his mood.

"My Lord," Nell said, "Is the food not to your liking?"

"Oh, forgive me, the meal is delicious; did you not like it? Should I ask to prepare anything for you?" Percival inquired worriedly, which irritated Nell. He hadn't even noticed. She huffed and returned to her meal without responding to him.

She should not be irritated with him; he must be fatigued. But he didn't even insist on being called Percival when she addressed him as my Lord. She has to be patient, but her heart will not listen.

"The food was very tasty, my Lord," Nell remarked when she finished. "I liked the cream ice very much."

Her smile was odd; Percival felt he had missed something, but he couldn't figure out what.

"Ah, yes, the cream ice, it is indeed good," Percival remarked cautiously.

They sat by the fire for longer than they did every day. Nell yanked Percival's wrist as he rose up to quit.

"Percival," she muttered, staring up at him, and he was entranced once again.

Percival did not say anything since he didn't trust his voice.

"Will you dance with me?" She inquired, gazing directly into his eyes, keeping herself from falling under his spell while attempting to draw him into hers, oblivious that he was long gone.

"Yes," he said feebly.

And they danced like they had the previous time, but this time it was more ethereal, a genuine daydream. There were no boundaries, no restrictions, and no one to stop them. They could do anything their heart desired. So, they did.

Nell was the first to kiss, which surprised Percival. She was never the one to express emotions so freely, and she never initiated intimacy, although being an enthusiastic participant. Hell, it was just the second time she kissed him alone.

"Nell," said Percival. "If you keep doing this, I won't be able to restrain myself."

Nell froze at his words and drew away.

Percival saw Nell suffering and kissed her forehead to comfort her. He walked her back to her rooms, knowing he couldn't sleep with her that night. He was startled and unsure of himself. He planned to put her into bed and spend the night in his room, restless. Oh, the torment! He sighed at the concept.

Before he could blink, Nell had closed the door to her room and kissed him again. Her room was drowning in darkness, only lighted by the faint glow of a fire in the hearth.

"You don't need to restrain yourself now," she whispered in his ear, sending a shudder down his spine.

She'd fallen asleep in his arms after making lovely love to him for the first time, causing him to lose his sensations and elevating him to the seventh sky.

But he understood that if one could get to the seventh sky, one could also go to the seventh hell.

He touched her cheek and said. "It seems like you're saying goodbye, Nell. I will not let you do that."

30

Chapter Thirty

"Are you sure you want to do this?"

"Yes, milord," Nell groaned.

Last night was great. She expected to lose certain aspects of herself, but instead she acquired something unique and unexplained. Something almost destroyed her determination to go, but as daylight arrived and she awoke in the chilly bed, she was reminded of who she was.

And now she was on her way to a location remote from him. The carriage wheel creaked on the pavement, and emptiness seeped into her heart. They'd been traveling for half a day, her heart accepting the gravity weighing on her and all that transpired in the morning blazing in her memory.

"I apologize, my dear. I wish I could stay in bed with you all day, but I had to go to the palace early today," Percival remarked, kissing her forehead as she rose from the bed. Her nakedness was concealed but yet exposed as he stood there in all his splendor, clothed beautifully as the ruler that he was.

He broke his fast with her in bed after helping her dress and checked on her well-being. He was in a rush, she could tell, so she seemed to be well and cheerful while her mind shouted that this was her new reality. Someday in the future, he will return to his wife in the morning, and even though he loves her, she will loathe herself.

So here she was, working with his youngest brother to help her flee the only world she saw for herself.

"Are you alright?" He overheard Dominic ask her.

Her instinctual response of "I am well" was stopped in her throat as she realized she was about to weep. She gathered herself and addressed Dominic with a kind smile and a conundrum in her mind.

"Why are you so kind to me?" She asked.

"What do you mean?" He asked again.

"We both know I could never marry him; I was always going to be someone lurking in the shadows. You could have left me fend for myself, but you gave in quickly when you promised to assist me in leaving," she stated gently.

He seemed to be mulling about her comments, and she could only expect his response would be easy riddance.

"No, I don't completely believe that you can't marry Percival," he said, his look perplexed and uncertain of his words. "My parents were a love match, and we'd always heard about their fairy tale romance. I saw a glimmer of the same love in you and Percival, but I had no idea love could be so tough. They made it sound so effortless." He stopped to consider, the vision of perfection in his imagination splitting up.

"Until you asked me for a promise to help you with your plan, I thought you'd have your fairy tale ending, but I'm not sure anymore," he replied boldly, gazing directly at her.

Before his comments could influence her, she rejected them. He was a spoiled little prince who had no concept of the difficulties that others encounter; he had the ability to live a dream life, and his words had no significance to her.

"I had no idea Lord and Lady Whitworth were in love," she murmured, brushing her feelings aside.

"It's quite the tale. My maternal grandpa was opposed to their marriage, but my parents stood together against it all," he stated cheerfully.

"Why would anyone be against their daughter marrying a Whitworth?" She inquired, puzzled.

Dominic chuckled heartily, confusing her even more.

"Well, if your daughter is a princess and can become a queen why would you want her to marry a man below her station and stay a lady?" He inquired between laughter.

Nell couldn't disguise her surprise; she knew the Whitworth family was related to royalty, but she had always assumed it was somewhere in their genealogy, not with their mother.

"Is that why Whitworth's are looked up as royalty?" She inquired, wanting to check that she was hearing correctly.

"Whitworths are the descendants of the first King, many of the Whitworths married into the royalty over the generations, my father was one of them," he said.

"If it happened over the generations why would your grandfather be opposed to the union?" She inquired, not knowing what was wrong.

"My grandfather is the youngest brother of the King and didn't quite like the other members of the royal family and my father being Crown Prince's confidant didn't sit well with him," he said.

Nell was overwhelmed by all of the information. The final spark of hope that made her wonder whether she was doing the right thing was extinguished. She'd never be accepted as a Princess' daughter-in-law.

"It is funny, though," Dominic said, grinning, ignorant of her mood.

"What is?" She asked reflexively.

"My father and the Crown Prince were not on good terms. They didn't even consider each other friends; they only had a responsibility to do, and my grandpa, unknowing of this, detested my father." He chuckled.

"But," Nell remarked, her uncertainty growing. She realized Percival never mentioned Prince either. Was it the same for him? Was everyone living with a feeling of responsibility? Was no one happy?

Nell wasn't sure how or who to ask these questions. She was going away from the one who would bring her happiness. She picked her own horrible existence, expecting Percival to be able to choose a life that would not be as bad as hers, but it seems that life does not spare anybody.

Nell delved further into her contradictory feelings. The conflict raging on within her would undoubtedly drive her nuts. She couldn't believe it felt worse than those days in imprisonment. If she didn't get a break soon, she'd probably hit her head against anything to stop thinking.

They left the estate in the morning, assuring Mrs. Fitzgerald that she would meet Mr. Davies and Hec at the orphanage, but it was already nightfall and she had no clue where Dominic was bringing her. The fear of the unknown was gradually setting in. In the midst of the excitement, she neglected to ask him where they were going, and her defenses were kicking in.

The carriage trip continued for a while, her attention fixed on Dominic the whole time, attempting to read him. The driver's unmistakable knock on the board instantly brought Dominic to his senses.

"Nell," Dominic said after a lengthy silence, "You have to forgive me."

She pictured the worst-case scenario that might happen to her. Lord, take compassion on her. Why did this happen to her every time she attempted to flee?

"I did not plan to do this to you, but Percival was all I could think about. My elder brother is my idol, and I can't see him broken like that again," he replied somberly.

Nell felt helpless.

"You promised me," she whispered, tears welling in her eyes.

"And I promised him too," he said gravely.

"Who?" She inquired, fearing the response.

"Percival!"

Time stopped for her.

Percival. She didn't get any of it. What the heck was going on here?

"I promised you I will help you leave whenever you wish," Dominic said, feeling her apprehension. "And I promise Percival that I will get you to him. He wanted me to kidnap you under false pretenses and bring you here."

Nell wanted to strangle the guy seated in front of him, whether he was Lord or not. How did things come out this way?

"There is a difference of one decision between my promise to him and you," He replied.

"What decision?" She inquired, struggling not to yell at him.

"We are at Gretna Green, and Percival is waiting for you in the town's church," he remarked somberly. "I promised to bring you to the church straight, but I also promised you to assist depart. I'll get down at the wayside pub, and the carriage driver will transport you anywhere you choose."

"Now, you have to decide if you want to go to him or go away."

31

Chapter Thirty-one

Percival was pacing in the church foyer. He had never visited Gretna Green. It was a rundown old town, and the sole cathedral, that welcomed couples with open arms, regardless of their position, stood proudly like a soldier. It was in no better shape than this sad town, yet it managed to keep its splendor among the wreckage.

Percival was unhappy when Dominic approached him at the palace and reminded him of Nell's desire to leave him. He felt like a failure, like his love wasn't enough to keep her with him, yet he couldn't let her go. He determined to spend his whole life to convincing her that she deserved to be loved, and he wanted her by his side.

He recognized that she had anxieties that he would never be able to grasp. Even if that was the case, he wanted to be at her side, hold her hand, and help her conquer her obstacles.

The priest and his wife were worried while waiting for his bride to arrive. Their initial concern changed to sympathy as they assumed the wife had abandoned him. Percival kept his gaze fixed on the road until he heard the definite sound of a carriage approaching; he held his breath as his brother's carriage came to a halt in front of the church.

He pushed forward to see what was causing the carriage to stop. His initial joy at Nell's reply faded as he stood in front of the closed carriage door and the driver informed him that Lord Dominic had abandoned them at the town's bar.

He knocked again on the door, hoping that it wasn't empty. He did not dare to open the door by himself. Percival must have stayed there for a lifetime, waiting for her to unveil herself. His life was going to alter forever, regardless of what was inside the carriage, emptiness or her.

The door creaked gently before opening to show an angry angel. He remained transfixed as she walked out, gazing at him disapprovingly.

"You kidnapped me," she exclaimed fiercely, jolting him out of his reverie.

He moved on and held her fiercely, melting into her. The smooth skin and form that fitted to him perfectly, exactly as the first time he had passed out in her arms.

"How dare you!" She replied, fighting against his grip as hot tears poured down her cheeks.

Percival wasted little time in pushing her toward the altar door. The guests stared warily at the exuberant groom and the tear-stained bride.

Percival stood alongside Nell, their hands interlocked, indicating the priest to begin the ceremony. When no one answered, Percival cast a reproachful glance at the priest.

"We require witnesses, milord," The priest coughed.

Percival temporarily forgot that his younger brother had abandoned him.

"Where is Dom?" Percival questioned Nell, "Had he not accompanied you? How could he leave you alone?" Nell laughed at his frustrated mood.

"Father, may I request your wife to be a witness?" Nell smiled, stunning everyone with her beauty.

"Definitely, and for the second witness, wife, I believe your mother could finally be of some use," the priest stated, causing his wife to frown at him. Soon after, an elderly lady joined them, hobbling with the assistance of a stick, and the woman pulled Nell to the corner.

"I have to ask, are you being forced or blackmailed to get married?" She asked.

"Does it count if my heart is being selfish while my brain thinks I am making a mistake?" Nell asked.

"The problem with our brain is that it overthinks at times, whereas our heart rarely fails us," she remarked, returning to the altar joyously.

"The marriage requires two witnesses to sign, my wife will sign and my mother-in-law needs to ask you some question before she approves you two to get married," he stated.

"I can speak for myself, ya, no need to butt in," The lady admitted to humiliating her family. "Now, young man, tell me if you have already compromised her?"

Percival blushed at the lady's candour. He glanced to Nell for assistance as she stood stunned.

"I love her," Percival said.

"Eh," The lady spoke with a loud voice.

"You need to speak up," The Priest said, "She hears higher."

"I love her, ma'am, and I swore in the house of God that I will always love her and keep her safe and happy," Percival replied earnestly in a louder tone.

"And you girl, are you certain he is not bluffing?" The lady turned to Nell, wiping away the slight smirk she had at Percival's expense.

She nodded to the lady.

"Ay, what are you waiting for now!" The lady shouted at the priest.

"Please state both of your names," the priest requested.

"Percival, and she is Nell," Percival said for both of them.

"Your full name and title, milord, as well as the lady's full name," the priest remarked, displeased.

"We are simply Nell and Percival and no one else," Percival whispered, gripping her hand as a tear streamed down her cheek. Her grin could not be hidden.

***

Percival was standing with his newlywed wife, who must be boiling within, and her face showed shame in front of everyone in the ballroom.

Her hand was comfortably buried in his grasp, and he gently traced circles on her palm, comforting her. This was an absurd concept from the start, but there was no better time to declare to everyone that he was married to the most gorgeous woman in London, if not all of Great Britain.

"Your Highnesses," Percival bowed to the Prince and Princess, while Nell attempted a respectable curtsy.

"Lord Whitworth," the Crown Prince recognized his buddy in the presence of the nobilities.

"I would like to introduce my wife, Lady Nell Whitworth," Percival stated with pride.

"Welcome to the Prince's ball, my Lady," the Prince said.

"You are so beautiful," the Princess said joyfully.

"A word, my Lord," The Prince urged Percival to follow him "alone."

Percival stood stiff, unwilling to leave Nell alone.

"Don't worry, I promise to protect her," the Princess reassured him.

He followed the Prince gently to a more isolated location.

"Please tell me that this is the final phase of my nightmare and that it will end soon," the Prince begged.

"When you promised you will find something more scandalous for the ton than this Spanish ball on the English land, I didn't expect it to be your wedding," the Prince went on to say.

"I am a terrible friend," The Prince sighed after a minute.

"That is true," Percival chuckled.

"This is not funny; the King's council will oppose you for this," the Prince stated worriedly.

"Then, I believe you will need to join the King's council without me," Percival replied, clapping his buddy on the back. He knew his privilege may be taken away from him, but just now all he could think about was Nell and how long the Princess would be able to hang on to her own.

"In hell, I will choose the King council over you," The Prince said, as Percival looked in the direction where they had left their spouses and saw the Princess alone, surrounded by the fake women.

"Before you barge toward my wife angrily, look over there," He heard the Prince divert his attention to the dance floor, where his wife seemed uncomfortable dancing with his younger brother Cedric as his family stood behind.

"And congratulations on the wedding," He concluded with the Prince's words to his bride, who stood on the opposite side, surrounded by his family.

32

Chapter Thirty-two

Nell was suffocating. The atmosphere in the parlour was enough to make anybody tremble in the corner, as the Whitworths emanated overwhelming strength. No one said anything since they returned to the Whitworth manor.

Everything occurred in a fog, overwhelmed by emotions. Fitzgerald's enthusiastically welcomed them back after their two-day excursion to Gretna Green as newlyweds. They spent days in bed making love to one another, and Percival persuaded her to attend Prince's Ball since it would be the finest venue to announce their marriage.

The ball was a nightmare in itself. When Percival instructed him to introduce the Lord and Lady of Whitworth, the footman stared at them, followed by the whole ballroom, which spoke about them. Everyone's prying gaze made her uneasy, but Percival's calming touch gave her the courage to face everything.

The Princess was incredibly charming; however, she couldn't tell whether she was honest when admiring her attractiveness. But when she had to leave Nell alone, everyone assaulted her more openly, claiming she was a mistress who would soon be thrown out. Their remarks and laughter made her screen crawl, and she wanted to go away.

She leaped from boiling water into the flames when Lord Cedric invited her to dance. She wasn't familiar with the ballroom regulations, but she knew she couldn't deny anybody a dance. The dance finished, and she found herself encircled by the Whitworth family, with Percival at the opposite end.

Percival moved quickly across the floor, greeting his parents and brother as was expected of them. They played the game as if they had practiced it hundreds of times in front of the public, and she was hardly given any part probably because she was a rookie to the theater.

Lord and Lady Whitworth moved to their majesties, while the other brothers elegantly danced on the floor after Dom had invited them to visit Whitworth Manor. She and Percival danced a few waltzes, and she realized it was all for show. When they returned to the mansion, everyone was there waiting for them.

Percival had gripped her hand since their carriage arrived at the manor's entrance, and he was still clutching her in his arms while waiting for others to speak up. Everyone continued looking at the green stone on her other hand, which was curled up in her skirt.

Whatever it was, she wanted it to be done with. The quiet was about to drive her crazy, and the memory of her kidnapping and days in prison made her tremble. Her breathing became laborious.

"This is unacceptable," Lady Seraphina remarked, her expression frozen. This was the worst; she wasn't sure which was worse: her separation from Percival or Percival's separation from his family as a result of her.

"Mother," Percival implored.

"We can't accept fleeing to Gretna Green and getting married like a thief for the Whitworth heir," She continued to ignore her son.

"I agree," Lord Whitworth said.

"We are sorry," Nell stated boldly, confronting the Whitworth straight. "We should have approached you and asked for your permission properly. We should have been more courageous and battled for our love."

She turned to Percival and squeezed his fingers closer.

"I believe in us, and I love you. Thank you," she said to him, smiling. He reflexively kissed the top of her head, eliciting a loud cough from Father Whitworth.

"You should have come to us," he said.

"Would you have accepted us or torn us apart?" She asked him.

"It would have depended on how much you fought to be with each other," he added, sitting near his wife.

"Now we can only do one thing," he said.

"We won't recognize this marriage," Lady Seraphina said.

She was unhappy, but she understood that all she needed was Percival, and other people's views didn't mean much.

"We will have a wedding befitting the heir to the Whitworth," Lady Seraphina stated comfortably. "Be prepared. I would go to any length to ensure the marriage of my first son."

"Welcome to the family, Nell," Father Whitworth said.

***

The next month flew by. Lady Seraphina had ordered them to reside in separate rooms as they prepared for their forthcoming wedding. The Gazette had come out against them, slandering them. Everyone kept the news from her, but after observing Lord Cedric, she knew it was horrible.

Everyone knew that nobilities with a vendetta against them for their money and power had aided and fostered even more rumors. The royal family's silence has given them the boldness to trash the oldest and most respected house in Great Britain.

Considering all of this, Lady Seraphina moved the site to St. Paul's Cathedral, claiming that the King owed her a favour and consented to her request. The cathedral was only open for royal family members' christenings and weddings, and the Whitworth wedding demonstrated the royal family's unequivocal recognition of Whitworth.

The Prince denied his seat on the King Council without his confidant, forcing the King Council to conform to the future King's desires. Nell had previously lived as a commoner, and she felt she lacked many qualities as a plain woman. With the assistance of Lady Seraphina, she began learning the ropes of aristocracy in order to become someone worthy of succeeding as Duchess of Whitworth and being an equal partner to Percival.

Lord Cedric was still furious over the union and avoided the manor as much as possible. The service personnel were warming up to her, and everything was gradually falling into place. She didn't allow her thoughts stray to the mayhem outside; she felt safe behind these walls.

The wedding day was coming. She was pleasantly surprised when Mr. Davies and Hec arrived to stay at the mansion; their reunion was like rejoining her father and brother after a long absence. The Donovans arrived at the manor a week before the wedding, with the younger Lord missing.

Lady Addie had instantly sought her out and insisted on becoming her bridesmaid, eventually making Nell her friend. Lady Addie intended to relocate to her parents' estate, which was under her uncle's care. Nell had no idea what had caused her to leave her home with Donovan, and she didn't know how to console her, so she ended up supporting her and saying she could rely on her.

Lord Octavian was an entirely different person, telling her she was now a part of the family and that he would do everything for her as he had for his brother. She was still a little terrified, but his nice nature was erasing his previous picture, and she thanked God she wasn't up against him.

Throughout the whole month, Percival courted her by giving her flowers and taking her on walks. Sneaking up to see her after Lady Seraphina had told him to stay away and cease disturbing her. He spoke to her about everything, making her feel comfortable enough to divulge her demons and gloom. He had taken her hand and kissed her gently. Everything was amazing. It was the happiest she'd ever been.

The wedding day passed in the blink of an eye, and she was going down the aisle with calm music playing and her gaze fixed on the ideal guy there waiting for her. She wanted to sulk because the groom couldn't turn around to look at her as she walked towards him, but even though she couldn't see his face, an invisible cord drew her closer.

She stood facing the priest, Percival at her side, and they shared a little grin.

"Dearly beloved, we have gathered here today in the presence of God to unite this man and this lady in holy marriage. If any man can prove any good cause why they may not be legally wedded together, let him now speak or else he must eternally keep his quiet." The priest hesitated.

Nell closed her eyes, hoping no one would yell scandal and ruin her sweet dream.

"Who giveth this woman to be married to this man?" The Priest inquired.

"I do," Mr. Davies said as he kissed Nell on both cheeks and put her hand on Percival's.

"I, Percival Montague Alden, take Nell to my wedded wife, to have and to hold, from this day forward, for better, for worse, for richer, for poorer, in sickness and in health, to love, cherish, and obey till death do us apart," Percival repeated, his voice resounding in the silent church as everyone held their breath.

"I, Nell, take Percival Montague Alden to my wedded husband, to have and to hold, from this day forward, for better, for worse, for richer, for poorer, in sickness and in health, to love, cherish and obey till death do us apart," Nell stated in a tranquil voice.

"The rings, please," replied the priest.

"Do you Percival Montague Alden Whitworth take thee, Nell Hawthorne, as your lawfully wedded wife?"

"I do," Percival said, placing the large green stone onto her finger.

"Do you Nell Hawthorne take thee Percival Montague Alden Whitworth as your lawfully wedded husband?"

"I do," Nell said, putting a freshly created white sparkling diamond onto his finger.

"With the power vested in me, I declare you husband and wife," The priest proceeded, "You may now kiss the bride."

The thundering ovation faded into the background as his lips touched hers, permanently connecting their hearts and souls.

Author Note

Thank you for reading my 4th book. This is standalone novel is Book 1 of 3. I would appreciate your honest opinion about the book in a review/suggestion for me to read.

Making my novels more appreciable to you is my top priority.

Thank you.

About the Author

Emily Higgs is a vibrant voice in the realm of fiction, weaving intricate tales that transport readers to captivating worlds. With a pen dipped in imagination and a mind brimming with creativity, she effortlessly spins narratives that enthrall and enchant.

Born with a passion for storytelling, Emily's journey as a writer began at a young age when she would pen short stories and poems, each one a glimpse into her boundless imagination. As she grew, so did her love for the written word, and she soon found herself immersed in the art of crafting novels.

Her characters are equally compelling, each one imbued with their own hopes, fears, and desires. From the reluctant hero embarking on a perilous quest to the enigmatic stranger hiding a dark secret, Emily's protagonists leap off the page, their journeys leaving an indelible mark on the reader's psyche.

Printed in Great Britain
by Amazon

40864024R00131